Gilmartin's
Word Study

By

John G. Gilmartin

Principal, Duggan and Begnal Schools
Waterbury, Conn.

Author of
Vocabulary-Building
and Practical English Course

SECOND REVISED EDITION

NEW YORK
PRENTICE-HALL, INC.
1941

First printing.............August, 1929
Second printing.............April, 1930
Third printing...............June, 1931
Fourth printing...........December, 1932
Fifth printing.................July, 1933
Sixth printing............February, 1934
Seventh printing..........September, 1934

REVISED EDITION

First printing.................May, 1935
Second printing............October, 1935
Third printing...........September, 1936
Fourth printing...........January, 1937
Fifth printing.................July, 1937
Sixth printing............December, 1937
Seventh printing.........September, 1938

SECOND REVISED EDITION

First printing......................April, 1940
Second printing.....................May, 1941

Preface

VOCABULARY–BUILDING is becoming more important each year, as is evidenced by the fact that many high schools and colleges are now making it an integral part of the English course.

Every person desires to be able to express himself fluently and accurately. That such a desire is not always an actuality is due largely to the scant attention given in the past to the subject of word study. One must admit that the ability to use a reasonably large vocabulary is absolutely necessary. The possession of such a vocabulary overcomes fear and self-consciousness, and supplants them with courage and self-possession. To insure the attainment of this objective is the primary hope and aim of the author.

The publication of the second edition of "Webster's New International Dictionary" has placed its stamp of approval on certain pronunciations which were formerly considered incorrect. "Word Study" conforms to these changes in usage, and will by its up-to-dateness and conformity to the usages of leading American dictionaries, be of great value to both teachers and students.

The author, in his selection of words, has utilized the leading and best sources obtainable, such as "Thorndike's Teachers' Word Book," better known as "Thorndike's 10,000 List." This list was prepared by Edward L. Thorndike, eminent psychologist, of Columbia University, after a study of millions of words taken from the Bible, compositions of pupils, letters, magazines, classics, and the newspapers. These were catalogued, and the 10,000 most frequently used words were arranged in the book according to their degree of frequency; that is, the first 1,000 appeared more often than those in the 2,000 position, and so on. The author has also consulted Jones's List, the Ayre-Buckingham Scale, and lists of words generally used in the leading business spellers. He made personal appeals to those in charge of secretarial forces in large business offices and factories in the Eastern states for lists of words often misspelled by those under their charge.

This book is very comprehensive in its contents, including not only extensive lists of words, with their definitions, and sentences showing their meanings, but also many lessons on correct usage and pronunciation. There is special consideration of prefixes and suffixes, words derived from foreign tongues, and words found in different lines of business. Lessons containing new methods of teaching, such as the completion test, the true and false test, and the multiple-choice test, are a feature.

This work contains more than 6,000 words, with many repetitions for the purpose of emphasis. This is, of course, rather too large a list for ordinary school use, but it affords the instructor a supply from which he may make a satisfactory selection.

At the end of nearly every lesson will be found questions or remarks pertinent to the lesson on that page, which should be a decided help to the student.

Not all words are defined or illustrated, as this might tend to alienate the pupil from the use of the dictionary. For the same reason, diacritical markings for pronunciation are not given in all cases, particularly when the word is amply familiar.

Throughout the book will be found tests related to the subject matter immediately preceding them. Each test covers approximately the work of one month.

The author wishes to express his gratitude to the many business firms which compiled lists of words commonly misspelled by their secretarial forces, and also to Mrs. J. G. Gilmartin and Helen Comstock for their valuable assistance in making the book a reality.

JOHN G. GILMARTIN.

Contents

To the Teacher

THE teacher should have a definite system for teaching spelling, if satisfactory results are to be obtained. Here are a few points which may be of value to the instructor:

When the spelling word is given, the pupils should visualize it, that is, see it with the mental eye, before they attempt to write.

Pupils should be taught to write subconsciously; they should not focus their entire attention on the words of the lesson. This end will be effected if the teacher will constantly dictate sentences that include the words of the day's or week's lesson. If this is done, the students will direct their attention to the sentence and not to the individual word. Dictation should be given preference to column spelling, as the students in post-high-school life will be called upon in their business employment to write sentences and not columns of words.

Insist that the pupils be able to use the words in oral and written sentences. This will result in augmented vocabularies. Stress the importance of correct pronunciation.

Pre-test System

The pre-test system is the system advocated by some of the leading educators of today.

On the first spelling day of the week, have the class write *without any preparation* all the words that will be given during the week. Correct the papers. Eliminate at once all those words which were spelled correctly by all the class, that is, the one hundred per cent words.

For the second day's lesson, the pupils should study only the words which they failed to spell correctly.

On the third day, the same list as the one first given, less all the one hundred per cent words of both days, should be dictated. Proceed then as on the second day.

The object of this system is to prevent the class from devoting time to words already known, thereby allowing more time for those words that cause difficulty.

INTRODUCTION

GUIDE TO PRONUNCIATION

The average pupil pays little, if any, attention to the vowel-markings found in every word. Although many rules may be given relative to the subject, this book will restrict itself to the more important signs.

ā	long	as in āte	ō	long	as in ōld
ă	short	as in căt	ŏ	short	as in stŏp
â	flat	as in râre	ȯ	medial	as in sȯft
ä	Italian	as in ärm	ô	broad	as in côrd
ȧ	medial	as in ȧsk	ō̇	modified long	as in ō̇bey
â	modified long	as in senâte			
			ōō	long	as in bōōt
ē	long	as in eat	ŏŏ	short	as in fŏŏt
ĕ	short	as in ĕdge			
ē̃	tilde	as in refē̃r	ů	modified long	as in valůable
e		as in they	ū	long	as in ūnit
ê	modified long	as in êvent	ŭ	short	as in cŭt
			û	circumflex	as in bûrn
ī	long	as in īce	ü	French	as in menü
ĭ	short	as in sĭn	ǔ	modified short	as in focǔs
ï	diaeresis	as in valïse			

SPELLING RULES

In arithmetic a rule must be followed: it rarely has an exception. But in spelling nearly every rule has many exceptions. This being the case, the most effective way for pupils to become efficient in the art of spelling is for them to memorize, not merely the rules, but the different words they meet.

Yet, notwithstanding the many exceptions to them, rules give a general knowledge of words that come under certain groups. It would be well, therefore, for pupils to familiarize themselves with them. The following are considered the most important:

RULE 1:

a. Words ending in final **e** usually drop the final **e** before a syllable beginning with a vowel: e.g., **ride, riding.** Exceptions are found in compounds taking the suffix **-able,** e.g., **marriageable, serviceable,** etc.

b. If the added syllable begins with a consonant, the final **e** is usually retained: e.g., **manage, management; peace, peaceful.**

c. If the word ends in double **e,** both **e's** are retained before a vowel or a consonant: e.g., **agree, agreeing, agreement.**

RULE 2:

Monosyllables and words accented on the last syllable, and ending in a single consonant preceded by a single vowel, double the final consonant before a suffix beginning with a vowel: e.g., **run, running; begin, beginning.**

RULE 3:

a. Words ending in **y** preceded by a consonant change **y** to **i** before a suffix not beginning with **i**: e.g., **enemy, enemies; family, families; ally, allies.**

b. If final **y** is preceded by a vowel, it is retained before a suffix: e.g., **valley, valleys; alloy, alloys.**

RULE 4:

Monosyllables ending in double **f, l,** or **s,** following a single vowel, generally retain the final consonant when a suffix is added: e.g., **will, willful.**

Rule 5:

Ei- and **ie-**combinations:

a. When these are sounded like **e, ei** is used after **c,** and **ie** after any other consonants: e.g., **receive, believe, grieve,** etc.

(Note: There are a few exceptions to this rule. Among these are: **leisure, seize, neither,** etc.)

b. When these are sounded like **ay, ei** is used: e.g., **reign, veil,** etc.

c. When these are sounded like long **i, ie** is generally used: e.g., **die, lie,** etc.

(Note: Exceptions are certain words ending in **-ght,** such as **height, sleight,** etc., and some foreign terms, such as **eiderdown.**)

d. When these are sounded like short **e** or **i, ei** is generally used: e.g., **heifer, foreign,** etc.

e. When these vowels are pronounced separately, **ie** is commonly used: e.g., **alien, patience,** etc.

RULES FOR USE OF THE HYPHEN

The hyphen is used:

1. When **ex-** precedes titles: e.g., **ex-president,** etc.

2. In spelled-out numbers below one hundred, when these consist of more than one word: e.g., **twenty-two,** etc.

3. When a numeral adjective precedes **-rate**: e.g., **second-rate,** etc.

4. Between the numerator and the denominator of spelled-out fractions used as adjectives: e.g., **three-fourths,** etc.

5. When certain adjectival expressions are compounded: e.g., **fair-haired,** etc.

RULES FOR FORMING THE PLURALS OF NOUNS

1. The regular rule for forming the plurals of most nouns is to add **s** to the singular. If the final letter of the singular does not unite in sound with **s** (as in the case of **x, z, ch, s,** and the like), add **es**.

boy	boys	box	boxes
horse	horses	church	churches

2. If a noun ends in **y** preceded by a consonant, the plural is formed by changing the **y** to **i** and adding **es**.

history	histories	daisy	daisies
city	cities	memory	memories

3a. If a noun ends in **o** preceded by a consonant, add **es** to form the plural.

echo	echoes	hero	heroes
tomato	tomatoes	potato	potatoes

(Some exceptions to this rule are: **pianos, solos, cantos.**)

b. To nouns ending in **o** preceded by a vowel, add **s**.

folio	folios	cameo	cameos

4. If a noun ends in **f** or **fe,** change the **f** or **fe** to **ves** to form the plural.

knife	knives	calf	calves

Some exceptions are:

dwarf	dwarfs	proof	proofs
safe	safes	scarf	scarfs
chief	chiefs	roof	roofs

5. Irregular plurals:

man	men	woman	women
mouse	mice	goose	geese
foot	feet	cherub	cherubim

6. Compound words:

In forming compound plurals, one should take care to distinguish the principal word, as it does not always occupy the same position. Usually only the principal word is changed to its plural form, as in:

son-in-law	sons-in-law	court-martial	courts-martial
man-of-war	men-of-war	poet-playwright	poet-playwrights

These, however, change in both parts:

Knight-Templar	Knights-Templars
man-servant	men-servants

7. Words ending in **ful** form their plurals by adding **s**.

spoonful	spoonfuls	pailful	pailfuls
mouthful	mouthfuls	handful	handfuls

8. Letters of the alphabet, numbers, and mathematical signs form their plurals by adding **'s**.

r's a's 4's 9's +'s x's

9. The following words have the same form in the singular and in the plural:

means	sheep	mackerel	series
athletics	ethics	wages	deer
politics	bellows	species	hose

10. Some words have two plurals whose meanings are different:

brother	brothers	(of a family)	brethren	(in a church)
head	heads	(of bodies)	head	(of cattle)
fish	fishes	(used separately)	fish	(used collectively)
cannon	cannons	(used separately)	cannon	(used collectively)

PLURALS OF FOREIGN WORDS

We have retained in our language many words whose singular and plural forms are the same as in the foreign language from which they were taken. Some, however, have been Anglicized in their plural forms.

Singular		*Plural*		*Singular Definition*
thesis	(thē′sĭs)	**theses**	(thē′sēz)	Essay.
datum	(dā′tŭm)	**data**	(dā′tȧ)	Fact.
basis	(bā′sĭs)	**bases**	(bā′sēz)	Foundation.
crisis	(krī′sĭs)	**crises**	(krī′sēz)	Turning point.
stratum	(strā′tŭm)	**strata**	(strā′tȧ)	Layer.
alumnus	(ă lŭm′nŭs)	**alumni**	(ă lŭm′nī)	Male graduate.
alumna	(ă lŭm′nȧ)	**alumnae**	(ă lŭm′nē)	Female graduate.
ellipsis	(ĕl lĭp′sĭs)	**ellipses**	(ĕl lĭp′sēz)	Omission.
hypothesis	(hī pŏth′ĕ sĭs)	**hypotheses**	(hī pŏth′ĕ sēz)	Supposition.
analysis	(ăn ăl′ĭ sĭs)	**analyses**	(ăn ăl′ĭ sēz)	Examination.
bacillus	(bă sĭl′lŭs)	**bacilli**	(bă sĭl′lī)	Germ.
diagnosis	(dī ăg nō′sĭs)	**diagnoses**	(dī ăg nō′sēz)	Investigation.

The following words have both a foreign plural form, and an English plural formed by adding **s**:

phenomenon	phenomenons	or phenomena
automaton	automatons	or automata
criterion	criterions	or criteria
cherub	cherubs	or cherubim

Lesson 1*

LATIN PREFIXES

A letter or syllable added at the beginning of a word to change its meaning is called a **prefix**.

Some Latin prefixes and their meanings follow:

Prefix	Meaning	Illustration
a, ab	From, away.	avert, abstain
ad, af, at	To.	adhere, affix, attain
ante	Before.	antedate, antemeridian
circum	Around, about.	circumference, circumnavigate
con, cor	With, together.	convene, correspond
contra, counter	Against.	contradict, counteract
de	From, down.	descend, debase
di	Apart.	divert, divorce
dis	Not.	disagree, dissuade
e, ex	Out of, from.	eject, exit
extra	Beyond.	extravagance
in, im, ir	Not.	inappropriate, impossible, irresponsible
per	Through.	permeate, percolate
post	After.	posterity, postpone
pre	Before.	predict, precede
pro	For, forth.	pronoun, procession
re	Back, again.	recall, revive
sub, subter	Under.	subordinate, subterfuge
super	Over, above.	superintendent, supervise
trans, tra	Across, beyond.	transport, traverse

Exercise

Give the root and the prefix for each of these words, and show how the prefix affects the meanings:

subscribe	subterranean	innumerable
concurrence	demoralize	perambulate
disappoint	commiserate	translucent
supernatural	excommunicate	extraordinary

*Lessons 1 to 3 may be omitted if the pupils have had no previous knowledge of the languages in question.

7

Lesson 2

GREEK PREFIXES

Inasmuch as the majority of words in the English language are derived from both Latin and Greek, it will be well to examine the more important Greek prefixes. Having compared the prefixes taken from both languages, you will readily see that a greater supply is obtained from the Latin.

Prefix	*Meaning*	*Illustration*
a, an	Without.	**atheist, anarchist**
ambi, amphi	Both, around.	**ambidextrous, amphitheater**
ana	Through.	**analysis**
ant, anti	Against.	**antonym, antipathy**
apo	From.	**apology**
cata	Down.	**catacomb, cataract**
dia	Through.	**diameter, diagnosis**
epi	Upon.	**epitaph, epigram**
hyper	Above, over.	**hypercritical, hyperbole**
hypo	Under.	**hypodermic**
meta	Beyond.	**metaphysical**
mono	One.	**monologue, monocle**
para	Similar.	**parable, parody**
peri	Around.	**perimeter**
poly	Many.	**polysyllable, polygon**
syn	With.	**syndicate, synonym**

Exercise

Give the word-root and the prefix of these words, and tell how the prefix affects the root:

amphibian	**paraphrase**	**synchronize**
epidemic	**synthetic**	**polychrome**
monosyllable	**periscope**	**hypersensitive**
hypocrite	**antiseptic**	**polytechnic**

8

Lesson 3

SUFFIXES

A **suffix** is a letter or syllable added to the end of a word or word-root to change its meaning.

Examples are:

able, ible	That may be; worthy of: movable, blamable, lovable, usable.
ac, al, ial	Pertaining to; of the nature of: cardiac, national, facial.
ance, ence	State of being: abundance, difference, obedience.
ant, ent	One who; that which: servant, student, superintendent.
er, or	One who: teacher, instructor, sailor.
ful	Full of: hopeful, helpful, skillful.
ish	Having the quality of: boorish, mannish, boyish.
ity	The quality of: servility, humility, ability.
ive	One who; that which: executive, sensitive.
less	Without: voiceless, restless, sleepless.
ly	Like: manly, cheerfully, lazily.
ness	State of: goodness, loneliness, holiness.
ous	Full of: anxious, joyous, ridiculous.
ry	State of: rivalry, discovery, ministry.

Exercise

Explain the prefixes and suffixes in:

transgress   digestible   illogical   antecedent

9

Lesson 4

SPELLING Ei- AND Ie-WORDS

1. When **ei** or **ie** has the sound of **ee**, the spelling usage may be discriminated as follows:

a. After **c** use **ei**: as in **ceiling, perceive, receive,** etc.

b. After any letter other than **c** use **ie**: as in **believe, grieve, reprieve,** etc.

(Exceptions: In **leisure, seize,** and **neither, ei** is used, though not following **c**.)

2. When sounded as **ay,** use **ei**: as in **sleigh, neighbor, weigh,** etc.

Exercise

State what rule, if any, applies to each of these words:

brief	niece	sieve	mischief
siege	pierce	friend	believe
priest	shriek	achieve	cashier
field	yield	frieze	kerchief
rein	veil	weird	receipt
freight	reign	either	conceit
weigh	neigh	leisure	height
sleigh	eighty	deceive	forfeit
aggrieve	glacier	weight	seizure
foreign	chief	fierce	skein
unveil	besiege	reprieve	seignior (yôr)
fiend	lieu	relief	feint
ancient	frontier	prairie	transient
deficient	mien	alien	seismic (sīs´-)
quotient	patient	wield	lieutenant
series	heir	adieu	convenient

10

Lesson 5

SPELLING Ei- AND Ie-WORDS

1. We have seen that, in the case of **ei-** and **ie**-words, when this combination of letters is sounded like **ee, ei** is used after **c,** and **ie** is used after any other consonants.

2. We have noted also that, when this combination of letters is sounded like **ay, ei** is used.

3. Finally, when it is sounded like neither of these, **ie** is generally used. There are a few exceptions to these rules, however. (See page 3.)

The following words show the regular usage:

Rule 1	*Rule 2*	*Rule 3*
reprieve	reign	patience
perceive	heir	sufficient
niece	vein	lie
piece	sleigh	friend

Exercise 1

Which of the following words are exceptions to the preceding rules?

convenient	(—yĕnt)	Adapted to one's comfort; handy.
inalienable	(—āl′yĕn à b'l)	That which cannot be taken away.
leisure	(lē′zhŭr)	Spare time at one's disposal.
seize	(sēz)	To take possession of by force; to grasp.
counterfeit	(—fĭt)	Spurious; bogus; not genuine.
grievous	(grēv′ŭs)	Causing sadness; painful; oppressive.
financier	(fĭn ăn sēr′)	One skilled in money transactions.
proficient	(—shĕnt)	Thoroughly qualified; skillful.
sovereign (*n.*)	(sŏv′ẽr ĭn)	Ruler, such as a king, emperor, or potentate.

Ei- and Ie-Words Used in Sentences

1. It is the **inalienable** right of every citizen to vote.

2. The **financier** was so occupied that he was unable to **seize a** moment's **leisure**.

3. The **sovereign** committed a **grievous** mistake in going to war.

4. Smith is the most **proficient** bridge-builder in the community.

Caution

Note that **alien** is pronounced **āl′yĕn,** and that **financier** is pronounced with a short **i** and with the accent on the last syllable.

Exercise 2

A. Write three words that end in **-ceive.**

B. Write two words in which **ei** has the sound of **ay.**

C. What rule applies to each of the following words?

ceiling	forfeit	achieve	transient
neighbor	mischief	weigh	foreign
sleigh	besiege	sieve	handkerchief

D. The following words are exceptions to what spelling rules?

pianos	proofs	height
leisure	scarfs	judgment
dwarfs	daily	hoofs
solos	weird	handkerchiefs

E. Can you find three mistakes in these sentences?

1. It is difficult to understand the phenomenas of nature.

2. We commented upon the greeness of the foliage.

3. John has finished his two theses.

4. I took two spoonsful of sugar.

Lesson 6

ABBREVIATIONS

Eng.	England	**masc.**	masculine
etc.	*et cetera;* and so forth	**mdse.**	merchandise
et al.	and others	**memo.**	memorandum
ex.	example	**mfg.**	manufacturing
Fla.	Florida	**mgr.**	manager
f.o.b.	free on board	**mtg.**	mortgage
ft.	foot	**misc.**	miscellaneous
fut.	future	**n.g.**	no good
Ga.	Georgia	**no.**	number
G. A. R.	Grand Army of the Republic	**p.** (plural, **pp.**)	page
geog.	geography	**pd.**	paid
gov.	governor	**pkg.**	package
govt.	government	**prox.**	*proximo;* next month
gr.	gross	**recd.**	received
ibid.	*ibidem;* in the same place or work	**sc.**	scene
id.	*idem;* the same	**sec.**	second; secretary
int.	interest	**ser.**	series
inst.	present month	**sts.**	streets
i.e.	*id est;* that is	**ult.**	*ultimo;* last month
lang.	language	**univ.**	university
led.	ledger	**viz.**	*videlicet;* namely
ltd.	limited	**via**	by way of
		wt.	weight

Exercise

What are the abbreviations for the following words?

bushel	doctor	general	major
afternoon	ounce	amount	before noon
debtor	junior	balance	pound
creditor	against	note well	postscript
reverend	manager	manuscript	for example

13

ABBREVIATIONS

A.B.	bachelor of arts	**cash.**	cashier
ad lib.	at pleasure	**chgs.**	charges
Ph.D.	Doctor of Philosophy	**coml.**	commercial
amt.	amount	**conj.**	{ conjunction / conjugation }
asst.	assistant		
acct.	account	**corp.**	corporation
ad inf.	*ad infinitum;* forever	**cr.**	credit
adj.	adjective	**Co.**	company
ad val.	*ad valorem;* according to the value	**cu.**	cubic
A.M.	*ante meridiem;* before noon	**cwt.**	hundredweight
		Del.	Delaware
		dept.	department
		dia.	diameter
anon.	anonymous	**dict.**	dictionary
assoc., assn.	association	**dist.**	district
ave.	avenue	**div.**	division
bal.	balance	**do.**	ditto
bk.	book	**doz.**	dozen
bldg.	building	**Dr.**	doctor; debtor
bro.	brother	**ea.**	each
bu.	bushel	**ed.**	{ edition / editor }
capt.	captain	**e.g.**	*exempli gratia;* for example
c/o	care of	**ency.**	encyclopedia

There is a movement on foot among educators to reduce the use of abbreviations to a minimum. Some recent works on grammar advocate the elimination of most abbreviations on envelopes, as in:

Mr. Thomas A. Nolan
1 Pequot Street
Waterbury
Connecticut

Lesson 8

BUSINESS TERMS

debtor	(dĕt'—)	One who owes something to another.
fugitive		One who flees from danger, duty, or other responsibility; a deserter.
voucher		A paper which bears witness to something; a receipt for payment.
executive (*n.*)	(ĕg zĕk'—)	An official or a body charged with carrying laws, policies, or other decisions into effect.
currency	(kûr'—)	Circulation; a medium of exchange, such as money or bank notes.
equable	(ē'kwà b'l)	Uniform; steady; even-tempered.
defaulter	(dĕ fôl'—)	One who fails in payment; one who fails to make an honest accounting.
recourse (*n.*)	(rē kôrs')	An appeal for aid or protection.
subsidize	(sŭb'sĭ—)	To help or encourage with financial aid.
recompense	(rĕk—)	To reward; repay; make amends for.
concession		Act of granting, as, for example, a point in dispute.
shrinkage	(—ăj)	The act of growing smaller in size; amount lost by contraction.
countersign	(—sīn)	An additional signature to a document to prove its validity.
ratify		Formally to approve of; to settle or confirm.
embargo		A government act forbidding commercial vessels to enter or leave a port.
trustee	(—tē')	A person to whom property or management of property is committed.
arbitration	(—trā'—)	Settlement of a question by mutual agreement; settlement of a dispute by persons chosen by both sides.
fiscal	(fĭs'kăl)	Pertaining to expenditures and financial affairs of a government.
actuary	(ăk'—)	An expert computer of insurance risks, and the like; official statistician of an insurance company.

15

Lesson 9

BUSINESS TERMS

allowance		Definite sum of money, or other means, granted.
notification	(—kā′—)	Act of giving information or warning.
livelihood	(līv′—)	Means of existence; regular support.
indorse	(ĭn dôrs′)	To write one's name on the back of; approve.
guaranty	(găr′—)	An assumption of responsibility for the performance of some obligation by another.
proceeds (n.)	(prō′—)	Money which results from a transaction.
vacancy	(vā′—)	State of being empty; a position open to applicants.
supervise	(—vīz)	To oversee; superintend.
business	(bĭz′nĕs)	Occupation; duty; affair.
margin		Difference between the cost and the selling price; also, in a brokerage house, a deposit of cash or stocks as security for money borrowed.

Meanings Illustrated in Sentences

accuracy		**Accuracy** in making change is necessary.
defray	(—frā′)	The principal will **defray** the expenses of the basket-ball team.
advisable		He deemed it **advisable** to sell his car.
commission		I received $100 **commission** on the sale.
punctual		Be **punctual** at business each day.
indebted	(—dĕt′—)	He is **indebted** to me for $10,000.

Exercise

1. Why is the **e** dropped in **advisable?**

2. What do the prefixes signify in these words: **defray, supervise, indorse, commission?**

3. Write five sentences that will contain the first ten words given above.

Ex.—To insure a better **livelihood** from your **business**, you must sell at a greater **margin**.

Lesson 10

MISCELLANEOUS WORDS

masticate	(măs′tĭ kāt)	To grind with the teeth; chew.
optimist	(ŏp′tĭ mĭst)	One who looks on the bright side of things.
venom	(vĕn′ŭm)	Matter which poisons or stings.
ordeal	(ôr′dĕ ăl)	A severe trial; test; experience.
massive	(măs′ĭv)	Weighty; heavy; bulky.
opportunity	(ŏp ŏr tū′nĭ tĭ)	Convenient time or occasion.
ventilate	(vĕn′tĭ lāt)	To supply with fresh air.
querulous	(kwĕr′ û lŭs)	Complaining; discontented.
luster	(lŭs′tẽr)	Sheen; brilliancy.
extempore	(ĕks tĕm′pŏ rē)	Without study or meditation.
vehement	(vē′hĕ mĕnt)	Very forcible; violent.
habitable	(hăb′ĭt á b′l)	Fit to live in comfortably.
expression	(ĕks prĕsh′ŭn)	A saying; mode of speech.
imitation	(ĭm ĭ tā′shŭn)ᵢ	That which is made to resemble something.
dictate (v.)	(dĭk′tāt)	To deliver a statement with authority.
fluent	(floo′ĕnt)	Eloquent; moving freely.
outrage	(out′rāj)	Gross insult or injury.
magnify	(măg′nĭ fī)	To make greater; exaggerate.
inference	(ĭn′fẽr ĕns)	That which is included or understood as a matter of course; conclusion.
exaggerate	(ĕg zăj′ẽr āt)	To enlarge beyond truth or reason; to overstate.

Exercise 1

1. Pronounce the following words:

debtor   **indorse**   **equable**   **dictate**

2. Give the adjectival form for:

venom   **accuracy**   **ratify**   **invitation**

3. To which words of the above list are these related?

extemporize   **habitation**   **dictation**
expressive   **vehemence**   **lustrous**

17

Exercise 2

1. Show how the prefix affects the meaning of: **infer, defer, refer.**

2. Are **query** and **querulous** derived from the same Latin word? Consult the dictionary for your answer.

Caution

Ordeal may also be pronounced: ôr dē'ăl.
Dictate may also be pronounced: dĭk tāt'.

Miscellaneous Words Illustrated

1. It is a healthful habit to **masticate** our food well.
2. You are an **optimist** even under unfavorable circumstances.
3. There was **venom** in his harsh criticism.
4. We are now going through the **ordeal** of poverty.
5. A **massive** new structure stands on the site of the old church.
6. Lunch time will give you an **opportunity** to **ventilate** the rooms.
7. I have little patience with **querulous** clients.
8. The **luster** of the metal had long ago disappeared.
9. It was difficult for him to speak **extempore.**
10. He denounced me in **vehement** language.
11. We entered a humble but very **habitable** home.
12. That **expression** is an **imitation** of Washington Irving.
13. You are in a position to **dictate** to us.
14. He had a **fluent,** quick way of speaking.
15. The **outrage** is bad enough; I do not care to **magnify** it.
16. My **inference** is that he was asked to resign.
17. I shall try not to **exaggerate** the facts.

Exercise 3

Write sentences containing these words:

optimism	expressive	vehemently
optimistic	expressible	vehemence
opportune	habitable	dictate
importune	habitat	dictation
importunate	habitancy	dictator
importunity	habitation	dictatorial

18

Lesson 11

BUSINESS TERMS

itemized	(ī′tĕm īzd)	Set down by separate entries, items, or particulars.
collateral	(cŏl lăt′ẽr ăl)	An additional obligation or security given for the payment of a note.
liquidate	(lĭk′wĭ dāt)	To pay off, as a debt.
nominal	(nŏm′ĭ năl)	Existing in name only; not actual.
remittance	(rĕ mĭt′ăns)	Sending of money, and the like; money sent back.
accumulate	(ă kū′mŭ lāt)	To pile up; amass; collect.
remuneration	(rĕ mū′nẽr ā′shŭn)	Compensation; pay; reward.
fluctuate	(flŭk′tŭ āt)	To rise and fall; to be undecided.
adjustment	(ă jŭst′mĕnt)	Bringing of affairs into proper condition.
syndicate (*n.*)	(sĭn′dĭ kăt)	An association to promote some enterprise, usually requiring much capital.
maturity	(mă tū′rĭ tĭ)	End of the period an obligation has to run.
accrue	(ă krōō′)	To be added as an increase or profit.
transcribe	(trăn skrīb′)	To write out a copy of matter dictated.
insolvent	(ĭn sŏl′vĕnt)	Unable to pay one's debts.
lucrative	(lū′krá tĭv)	Profitable; gainful.
transaction	(trăns ăk′shŭn)	A business dealing.
mercenary	(mûr′sĕ nă′rĭ)	Acting only for reward or money.
temporary	(tĕm′pŏ rá′rĭ)	Not permanent; limited.
consolidate	(kŏn sŏl′ĭ dāt)	To combine; to strengthen.
appraisement	(ă prāz′mĕnt)	Estimated value of property.
integrity	(ĭn tĕg′rĭ tĭ)	Honesty; uprightness.
clientele	(klī ĕn tĕl′)	Clients collectively; those who go to a person for professional advice.

19

Lesson 12

BUSINESS TERMS ILLUSTRATED

deficit	There was a **deficit** of $1,000 in my business last month.
clerical	We have a shortage of **clerical** help in our office.
assets	To be successful in business, one must have **assets** that exceed his liabilities.
withdrawal	The bank passbook showed a **withdrawal** of $200 on February 15.
payable	Make the check **payable** to my brother.
retail	The **retail** price was twenty per cent greater than the wholesale price.
warehouse	It will be necessary to build a large **warehouse** for our goods.
statistics	**Statistics** proved that more people died of influenza than were killed in the war.
panic	Fear of a **panic** forced many depositors to withdraw their funds.
revenue	The state receives an immense **revenue** from autoists.
customer	The **customer** was displeased with the clerk's treatment.
schedule	Trains do not always run on **schedule**.
postage	The letter did not have sufficient **postage**.
industrial	All **industrial** plants will close on Thanksgiving Day.
mortgage	I raised a $5,000 **mortgage** on my house.
preferred	The company refused to sell any **preferred** stock.
surplus	They voted to use the **surplus** money to purchase new machinery.
creditor	The **creditors** lost much money when Brown and Company went into bankruptcy.
receipts	Our **receipts** last year were $1,000,000.
resignation	The secretary has sent in his **resignation**.
compensation	For the loss of his leg he received $2,000 **compensation**.
representative	I did not meet any **representative** from the City Bank.
memorandum	Kindly make a **memorandum** of what takes place at the meeting.

Lesson 13

BUSINESS TERMS
Multiple-Choice Exercises

A. Select the correct meaning for each word from the three meanings given:

dividends		(1) debts, (2) returns on investments, (3) stock.
conservator	(—vā—)	(1) lawyer, (2) custodian, (3) client.
bullion	(bŏŏl′yŭn)	(1) uncoined gold, (2) a number, (3) soup.
ultimo	(ŭl′tĭ mō)	(1) this month, (2) last month, (3) next month.
resources	(—sôr′sĕz)	(1) liabilities, (2) available means, (3) debts.
commodity	(—mŏd′—)	(1) something that is bought or sold, (2) warehouse, (3) money.
usury	(ū′zhŭ—)	(1) excessive interest, (2) tax, (3) merchandise.
consignee	(—sĭ nē′)	(1) one to whom goods are shipped, (2) the goods, (3) one who sends the goods.
industry	(ĭn′—)	(1) occupation, (2) place of business, (3) business.
discrimination		(1) unfair distinction, (2) crime, (3) deceit.
rescind	(—sĭnd′)	(1) to permit, (2) annul, (3) cut.
solicit	(—lĭs′—)	(1) to ask, (2) allow, (3) steal.

B. Which of the two words in parentheses is the appropriate form?

1. Five (**nickles, nickels**) make a quarter.
2. The (**stipulation, compensation**) was that I should pay the bill in one year.
3. There is keen (**boycott, competition**) in every trade.
4. A (**financier, inventor**) is a person who is skilled in finance.
5. I was unable to cash the check, as there was no one in the bank who could (**identify, rectify**) me.
6. The charge against the cashier was (**defalcation, dishonesty**) of the funds of the bank.

21

TEST I

(This test embraces the material found in Lessons 1–13, inclusive.)

I. Write the plurals of:

valley	echo	spoonful	athletics
ethics	dwarf	tomato	son-in-law
knife	4, a, x,	brother	court-martial
datum	thesis	alumna	diagnosis

II. Are the bold-type words correctly used?

1. The Senate refused to **ratify** the treaty.
2. He found it **very** difficult to **liquidate** his debts.
3. Mr. Condon has **accumulated** a large fortune.

III. Name five suffixes. Illustrate each.

IV. Which of these **ie-** and **ei-**words are incorrectly spelled?

brief	sieve	weird	mischief
seige	reign	relieve	deficient
perceive	foreign	sieze	patience

V. Give the meanings of these prefixes:

ab	ante	amphi	post	super
dia	peri	anti	syn	contra

VI. Write a word related to each of the following:

optimist	inference	habitable
punctual	supervise	competition

VII. Construct sentences containing:

rescind	payable	solicit
advisable	fluctuate	lucrative

VIII. How are these words pronounced?

ordeal	schedule	mortgage
deficit	dictate	recourse

22

Lesson 14

BUSINESS TERMS

dissolution	Act of breaking up.
assignment	Act of appointing or allotting.
countersign	To sign in addition to the signature of another.
appraisal	Act of setting a value on.
compromise	A settlement reached by mutual concessions.
negotiable	Transferable in the ordinary course of business.
defunct	Dead, deceased.
ascertain	To make certain to the mind.
exorbitant	Going beyond established limits.
procedure	Progress, conduct.
catalogue	A list.
lucrative	Profitable.
anonymous	Nameless.
speculator	One who engages in a transaction for the chance of a large profit.
genuine	Authentic, not false or counterfeit.
indicative	Pointing out, suggestive.
stringency	Lack of available money.
discrepancy	Difference or variance.
customary	Habitual.
redeemable	Capable of being recovered by payment of what is due.
pecuniary	Relating to money.
approximate (*adj.*)	Approaching correctness; nearly exact.
solvency	Ability to pay all just debts.
inestimable	Above all price or valuation.
systematize	To reduce to method; to methodize.

Cautions

1. The pronunciation of genuine is jĕn′û ĭn, not jĕn′ū īn.
2. Pecuniary is a word of five syllables.

23

Words Illustrated

The words given in the preceding section are here illustrated:

1. **Dissolution** of the firm followed the bankruptcy.
2. My **assignment** was to canvass the neighborhood.
3. I was asked to **countersign** the agreement.
4. Everything was considered in the **appraisal** of the property.
5. At last a **compromise** was reached.
6. The debt was paid by the sale of **negotiable** bonds.
7. The property of the **defunct** went to the state.
8. It was difficult to **ascertain** the truth of the case.
9. He paid an **exorbitant** price for the building.
10. The legal **procedure** was long and tiresome.
11. The articles for sale were listed in a **catalogue.**
12. The work was interesting but not **lucrative.**
13. He expressed his ideas in an **anonymous** letter.
14. As a **speculator,** he lost and made large sums.
15. The document was declared to be **genuine.**
16. The scarcity of sugar was **indicative** of a rise in price.
17. The **stringency** of finances was causing uneasiness.
18. There is not a great **discrepancy** between your account and mine.
19. It is **customary** for him to walk home every evening.
20. Five hundred dollars will **redeem** your property.
21. Mr. Gregory promised any **pecuniary** aid that was necessary.
22. The **approximate** value of the jewels was $10,000.
23. The firm, though in financial distress, was **solvent.**
24. Your assistance to me is **inestimable.**
25. Let us so **systematize** our work as to take the least possible time.

Exercise

1. Explain the **dis** in **dissolution** and **counter** in **countersign.**

2. Give the verb-forms of:

indicative   redeemable   negotiable

3. Use in sentences:

     exorbitant demands   pecuniary losses
     lucrative undertaking   approximate cost

Lesson 15

WORDS FROM THE AYRE-BUCKINGHAM SCALE

The following words are some of those found in the Ayre-Buckingham Scale. The per cent at the top of each list indicates the percentage of the words that a freshman high-school class should spell correctly without any preparation.

94%	92%	88%
circular	whether	testimony
argument	probably	evidence
absence	foreign	principal
entitle	responsible	experience
comrade	elaborate (*adj.*)	reference
anxious	ceremony	secretary
design	achieve	desirable
whistle	distinguish	extremely
sleigh	grateful	leisure
saucer	ignorance	occasion
biscuits	delicious	apparent
really	reverence	welfare
commerce	musician	individual
genuine	disappear	campaign
electricity	necessary	independent
investigation	rehearse	mysterious

After the class has been tested on these words in column spelling, it will be well to ascertain the results when the same words are dictated in sentences. To this end, sentences such as the following, each containing two or three words from the preceding groups, may be constructed:

The **secretary** found it **necessary** to ask for **references** from new members.

The **principal** is making **elaborate** plans for the occasion.

Lesson 16

BUSINESS TERMS

corporation (kôr pŏ rā´—)	A stock company formed to engage in commercial or other activities.
signature	Name of a person written by himself.
indorsement	Act of writing on the back of a note, check, bill, or other commercial paper; approval.
installment (or **instalment**)	Partial payment made for goods at a stated time.
secretary (sĕk´rĕ tă´rĭ)	One who attends to correspondence, arranges appointments, takes notes, and so forth.
inventory	An itemized list of goods, with their estimated worth.
liabilities	Debts, taken collectively, as opposed to assets.
reasonable	Not excessive; just.
wholesale	In large quantities; widespread.
profitable	Gainful.
resources (rĕ sôr´sĕz)	Money; property; skill.
employee	One who is in the employment of another.
bankruptcy	Complete failure of financial or other resources.
enterprise	An undertaking; a venture.
overhead (n.)	The general costs of running a business.
capitalist	A person controlling much wealth which is, or may be, used to promote business.

Some of the words from the preceding list are here used in sentences:

1. The automobile was paid for in forty-dollar, monthly **installments**.
2. Mr. Hayward's new enterprise has proved very **profitable**.
3. The man went into bankruptcy because his **liabilities** were far greater than his assets.
4. An up-to-date concern takes an **inventory** at least once a year.
5. His speech did not receive the **indorsement** of his superior officers.

Lesson 17

BUSINESS TERMS

I	II	
discount	solicit	To ask, to request.
cashier	audit	To examine or investigate.
debtor (dĕt—)	depositor	One who puts money in a bank.
ledger	invoice	Itemized statement of goods bought.
capitalist	negotiate	(—gō′shǐ—) To make a bargain, to transfer.
employee	merchandise	Goods, wares.
partner	consignee	(—sī nē′) One to whom goods are sent.
investment	appraisal	A valuation, estimate.

Business Terms Illustrated

1. The **invoice** of the **merchandise** was given to the **consignee**.
2. The **capitalist** refused to make an **appraisal** of his **partner's** property.
3. The **employee** tried to **negotiate** a loan with which to pay for his house.
4. A state agent will **audit** the **cashier's** books on the first day of every month.

Exercises

bonus	bankrupt	accuracy
currency	contraband	usury
liabilities	syndicate	revenue
warehouse	fraudulent	defray

A. Which of the preceding words have the following meanings?

1. To bear the expense of.
2. Unlawful interest.
3. Forbidden goods.
4. Payment as a premium.
5. Storehouse for goods.
6. That which is used as money.
7. Dishonest, tricky.
8. Debts, financial bills.
9. Exactness, correctness.
10. Combination of capitalists.

B. Place each of these expressions in a sentence:

fraudulent act	audit the books
defray expenses	contraband goods

27

Lesson 18

BUSINESS WORDS FREQUENTLY MISSPELLED

In an endeavor to procure a list of those words which are frequently misspelled by secretarial and office workers, the author sought the help of the heads of many business houses and organizations. Here are reproduced a few examples:

gauge	Often incorrectly written **guage**.
seize	
loose	Often confounded with **lose**.
cite—site	Frequently misused.
led	Misspelled **lead**.
there—their	Confused, owing to carelessness.
relevant	Many times misspelled **revelant**.
all right	Never **alright**.
stationary (*adj.*) stationery (*n.*)	Clerks find it hard to distinguish between these two words.
parallel	The tendency is to double the last **l**.
loath (*adj.*) loathe (*v.*)	The verb is never written **loth**.
consensus	Never **concensus**.
questionnaire	Often misspelled **questionaire**.
changeable	The **e** is often omitted.
accommodate	One **m** is often omitted.
accumulate	Misspelled with two **m**'s.
embarrass	Misspelled with one **r**.
scrapped	Often incorrectly spelled **scraped**.
principal	Often misspelled **principle**.
stripped	Often incorrectly spelled **striped**.
privilege	Never **priviledge**.
its (*possessive*)	Often misspelled **it's**.
lightning	Not **lightening**.
lath (*building material*)	Often confounded with **lathe,** a machine.
affect—effect	The misuse of these words is common.
advice—advise	These seem to be often interchanged.
receive	Carelessness about the **ie-** and **ei-**rules.
similar	Often misspelled **similer**.
occurrence	There is a decided tendency to drop one **r**.
inflammable	Many do not remember to double the **m**.
susceptible	Not **susceptable**.

Lesson 19

WORDS SUBMITTED BY BUSINESS HEADS

Other words which are often misspelled by office employees
are the following list, submitted by heads of business enter-
prises:

socks	believe	magazine
blocks	scissors	atomizer
budget	sachet	unguent
grippe	apparel	separate
satchel	apropos	cretonne
charmeuse	linoleum	negligee
mortgage	axminster	congoleum
nuisance	practically	appreciate
pajamas	percolator	opportunity
marabou	marquisette	mercurochrome
procedure	auxiliary	feasible
counsel (attorney)	resiliency	metallurgical
symmetrical	possession	excerpt
maintenance	committee	ceiling
iridescent	lie, lying	exercise

Correct Form	*Misspelled Form*
liquefy	liquify
kimono	kimona
chamois	shamois
business	bizness
belief	beleif
privilege	privelege
subsidiary	subsidary
paraffin	parafin
grievance	greivance
assessment	assesment
arrangement	arrangment
spoonfuls	spoonsful
advertisement	advertizement
hemorrhage	hemorage

29

Lesson 20

MISCELLANEOUS WORDS WITH COMPLETION EXERCISES

Exercise 1

assurance	Confidence; pledge.	**bondage**	Subjection.
meditate	To think upon; to plan.	**rebuke** (*n.*)	A sharp reproof.
caress	To embrace; to fondle.	**conscious**	Aware; sensible.
fetter	To bind; to restrain.	**abolish**	To put an end to.

Fill each blank with an appropriate word taken from the preceding list:

1. I received a severe _____ for my tardiness this morning.
2. John stopped to _____ the child he met.
3. One of the aims of education is to free us from _____ to superstition and incorrect thinking.
4. We received the _____ that our request would be granted.
5. He was always _____ of the ties that _____ him.
6. It is well to _____ before we act.

Exercise 2

regulate	To put in proper order.	**stricken**	Wounded; worn out.
flattery	False praise.	**reality**	Fact; truth.
solitary	Lonely; single.	**constrain**	To urge; to compel.
adversary	An enemy; a foe.	**amazement**	Wonder; surprise.

Fill each blank from the list of words given above:

1. James's _____ had the better of him on this point.
2. Mrs. Lawrence was never _____, for she had hosts of friends.
3. The _____ of his acting was the admiration of all.
4. We were _____ with _____ at the audacity of his manner.
5. I was _____ to forbid them to enter the house.
6. It is well to _____ our work so as to accomplish as much as possible.
7. Gerald knew that these words were mere _____.

Lesson 21

WORDS OF THE 5,500–6,000 POSITION
IN THORNDIKE'S LIST[1]

cautious	Exercising discretion; careful.
fidelity	Faithfulness; careful regard for duty.
impulse	A force that urges forward; temporary strong feeling inciting to some act.
modesty	Regard for what is decent and proper; lack of conceit.
faction	A group of persons united against others for a common purpose.
incapable	Deficient in ability.
augment	To increase in any way.
navigable	Capable of being traveled over by a boat or ship.
infirmity	Weakness of body or mind; unsteadiness.
authorize	To give a right to act or command.
plaintiff	One who begins a suit in court.
transgress	To break a law or rule; to exceed some limit.
compromise	The settlement of any dispute by which both parties give up part of what they first demanded.
injurious	Hurtful, physically or morally.
available	Attainable for one's purpose; at hand.
innumerable	Incapable of being counted; numberless.

Exercise

To which of the preceding words are the boldface words below related?

1. He was very **modest** about his success.

2. His **impulsive** temper has often proved a great obstacle to him.

3. There were **numerous** gatherings during those years.

4. One should **avail** himself of every opportunity afforded.

5. Did you hear the complaint of that **infirm** man?

6. Under whose **authority** did Magellan **navigate** the seas?

[1] For the meaning of this and similar terms, see the Preface, where there is a description of the Thorndike Word List.

Lesson 22

EXERCISES

A. Can you find eight mistakes in spelling in these sentences? Not every sentence contains a mistake. The misspelled words have been given in previous lessons.

1. More emphasis should be placed upon the importance of correct pronounciation.
2. I deem it a priviledge to be able to address my fellow men.
3. Many times our judgments are too severe and unecessary.
4. Each classroom has an ample supply of referrence books for the pupils' use.
5. My brother's independant attitude embarassed me very much.
6. In our high-school classes the boys are separated from the girls.
7. I spent two months during last vacation with an old acquaintence.
8. Undoubtedly Mr. Kennedy will be the new street superintendant.
9. He was hoping his team would win.

B. There are many words which we can spell correctly and with ease, but which we do not often use in written or oral work. Construct sentences with each of the following words:

punctual	Prompt, done at the exact time.
boundless	Without limits, vast.
novelty	The quality of being new, a change.
denote	To signify, to indicate, to mark out plainly.
assignment	An allotment; a thing designated as a lesson.
suitable	Becoming, fitting, appropriate.
ordinance	A law or statute.
primarily	In the first place, essentially.

Cautions

Do not confound **ordinance** with **ordnance,** a military word which means heavy warfare guns or military supplies.

It is now correct to say **prī mâr′ĭ lĭ** or **prī′měr ĭ lĭ.**

Question

Is **infinite** a synonym for **boundless?**

LEGAL TERMS

testify		To bear witness; to make a formal declaration; to serve as witness.
injustice		Quality of being unfair; an injury.
evidence		Testimony; proof.
trespass	(trĕs'—)	To enter unlawfully upon the property of another.
barrister	(băr'—)	An attorney; one who prepares the case.
plaintiff		One who begins a suit in court.
attorney	(ă tûr'—)	A legal representative.
defendant		A person who is sued or accused.
discharge (v.)	(—chärj')	To set free from restraint or custody.
testimony		Declaration by a witness under oath.
prosecute		To bring suit against in a court of law; to attempt to obtain a claim by law.
counsel		An advocate or attorney; advice.
statute		A law passed by an authorized lawmaking body.
verdict		Decision; judgment; opinion.
notary	(nō'—)	An official appointed by law to acknowledge deeds as contracts.
affidavit	(—dā'—)	A written statement to the truth of which an oath is taken before an authorized officer.
document		A record; an official paper, such as a deed.
versus	(vûr'—)	Against.
penalty		Legal punishment for breaking a law; a fine to be paid.
legislation	(lĕj ĭs lā'—)	Act of making laws; the law made by a legislative body.
valid	(vă'—)	Based on fact; sound; legally sufficient.

Caution

Distinguish carefully between: **counsel** (n.), meaning advice or an attorney; and **council** (n.), meaning an assembly for consultation or a legislative body.

Lesson 24

LEGAL TERMS

vindicate		To defend successfully; to free from suspicion; to prove just.
perjury	(pûr'—)	Willful assertion of a fact, made under oath, with knowledge that it is false.
duress	(dū'—)	The compelling of another to do something by threat or violence.
irrelevant	(ĭr rĕl'—)	Not applicable.
rescind	(rē sĭnd')	To annul; to make void; to repeal.
culpable	(kŭl'—)	Deserving censure or blame.
lenient	(lē'nĭ ĕnt; lēn'yent)	Not strict; mild; merciful.
nullify	(—fī)	To render void or invalid.
arbitrary	(—tră—)	Despotic; unreasonable.
infringement		A trespass upon a right, patent, or other privilege belonging to another.
allegation	(—gā'—)	Positive assertion.
illegal	(—lēg'—)	Unlawful.

Exercise

Fill the blanks with appropriate words taken from the preceding list:

1. An attempt was made to _____ the verdict.
2. The judge considered the testimony _____ to the case and would not admit it.
3. Mr. Brown was held _____ of the crime.
4. An oath under _____ is not binding.
5. I believe it is better for a lawyer to be a little _____ than too _____.
6. The _____ was that there was an _____ upon his patent.
7. Mr. Alexander endeavored to _____ his connection with the oil scandal.
8. In some states, to play baseball on Sunday is _____.
9. The witness was found guilty of _____ and sent to jail for thirty days.
10. The many good acts he performed were somewhat _____ by his boasts.
11. _____ means were used by the detective to elicit a confession of guilt from the man.

WORDS OF THE 4,000–5,000 POSITION IN THORNDIKE'S LIST

censure (*n.*)	(sĕn'shŭr)	An expression of disapproval; reproof.
illustrious	(ĭ lŭs'trĭ ŭs)	Renowned; famous; honored.
oppression	(ŏ prĕsh'ŭn)	Tyranny; that which burdens; hardship.
solitude	(sŏl'ĭ tūd)	State of being by oneself; seclusion.
hostile	(hŏs'tĭl)	Adverse; unfriendly.
signify	(sĭg'nĭ fī)	To make known; to declare; to denote.
inevitable	(ĭn ĕv'ĭ tả b'l)	Not to be evaded; unavoidable.
vanquish	(văn'kwĭsh)	To conquer; to subdue.

Exercises

A. Fill each blank with an appropriate word taken from the preceding list:

1. Washington, Jefferson, and Madison were the most _____ men of the Revolutionary period.
2. No longer do _____ relations exist between England and the United States.
3. The early settlers in America found it difficult to _____ the Indians.
4. Pupils who idle away their time in and out of school will be _____ failures in life.
5. The President did not _____ his intention of coming here for the opening of the new bridge.
6. Many persons prefer the _____ of the country to the din and noise of the city.
7. Did the executive _____ Jones for the rash remark he made concerning the firm?
8. The peasants lived under the yoke of _____ for many long years.
9. Much _____ was heaped upon him for his mistake.

B. Construct sentences including the following words:

significant	hostility	solitary
inevitably	oppressed	censorious

Lesson 26

LEGAL TERMS

behavior	(bē hāv′yẽr)	Conduct; manners.
advocate (*n.*)	(ăd′vō kăt)	One, such as a lawyer or counsellor at court, who pleads the cause of another.
litigant	(lĭt′ĭ gănt)	Either party in a lawsuit.
exemption	(ĕg zĕmp′shŭn)	Freedom from a duty or obligation.
repeal (*v.*)	(rē pēl′)	To cancel or annul; revoke.
incriminate	(ĭn krĭm′ĭ nāt)	To accuse or to involve in a crime.
acquittal	(ă kwĭt′ăl)	Legal decision freeing a person accused.
replevin	(rē plĕv′ĭn)	To get back, by an order of court, wrongfully seized goods.
proxy	(prŏk′sĭ)	A person appointed to represent another.
arraign	(ă rān′)	To call to account; accuse.
quasi	(kwā′sī; kwä′sĭ)	Almost; seemingly; as if.
illicit	(ĭ lĭs′ĭt)	Unlawful.
adjure	(ă jōōr′)	To charge or command solemnly; entreat earnestly.
libel	(lī′bĕl)	Statement which reflects upon the character of another without justification.
archives	(är′kīvz)	A place where public or state records are kept.
docket	(dŏk′ĕt)	List of cases for trial.
bailiff	(bāl′ĭf)	Chief magistrate; a sheriff's officer or constable.
assessor	(ă sĕs′ẽr)	One appointed to estimate the value of property for taxation.
heritage	(hĕr′ĭ tăj)	An estate that passes by descent.
legitimate	(lē jĭt′ĭ mĭt)	Lawful.

Exercise

1. Construct a sentence using **advocate** as a verb.
2. What is an antonym for **legitimate**?
3. Distinguish the spellings of the two synonymous words **illegal** and **illicit**.
4. From what verb is **litigant** derived?

36

Lesson 27

LEGAL TERMS ILLUSTRATED

absolve	Did the judge **absolve** him of all connection with the crime?
incorporate	The two leading law firms of the city have decided to **incorporate**.
liquidate	The merchant has promised to **liquidate** his debts within a year.
heinous (hā'—)	To steal from the poor is a **heinous** offense.
breach	The charge against the man, who publicly used profanity, was **breach** of the peace.
alimony (—mŏ—)	Jones was ordered to pay his wife ten dollars a week **alimony**.
validity	The **validity** of the lawyer's argument won the case for his client.
amenable (—mē'—)	A good judge is always **amenable** to reason.
jurisprudence	A thorough knowledge of **jurisprudence** is essential to a successful lawyer.
custody	The orphans were placed in the **custody** of their kind uncle.
quash	An attempt was made to **quash** the lawsuit.
trespass	To **trespass** upon railroad property is punishable by the court.
precedent (prĕ'—)	To be too easy with speedy autoists would be establishing a bad **precedent**.
ejection	The **ejection** of the tenant was due to his failure to pay his rent.
bequest	One of the many **bequests** made by Mr. Smith was a dormitory for his Alma Mater.

Exercise

Construct sentences containing these words:

precede	(prĕ sēd')	To go before in time, place, or rank.
precedent	(prĕ'sĕ dĕnt)	A rule established by previous action; a model.
precedence	(prĕ sē'dĕns)	The act of going before; superiority in rank.

MISCELLANEOUS WORDS

erroneous	(ĕr rō'nĕ ŭs)	False; misleading.
pertinent	(pĕr'tĭ nĕnt)	Relating to the subject in question.
influential	(ĭn flōō ĕn'shăl)	Having, or exerting, power or influence.
plaint	(plānt)	Utterance of grief aloud; a complaint.
redeem	(rē dēm')	To buy back; to free from bondage, sin, or other unfortunate state.
genial	(jē'nĭ ăl)	Kindly and sympathetic in disposition.
beautify	(bū'tĭ fī)	To make charming; to adorn.
condone	(kŏn dōn')	To pardon or overlook some act or fault.
behavior	(bĕ hāv'yĕr)	Conduct; deportment.
generosity	(jĕn ĕr ŏs'ĭ tĭ)	Quality of being liberal.
record (*n.*)	(rĕk'ĕrd)	An account of; an official writing.
placate	(plā'kāt)	To appease; to make friendly; to conciliate.
conference	(kŏn'fĕr ĕns)	A meeting appointed for discussing some topic or business.
flourish	(flûr'ĭsh)	To prosper; to thrive; to be vigorous.
jovial	(jō'vĭ ăl)	Jolly; merry.
conclude	(kŏn klōōd')	To bring about as a result; to come to an end; to determine.
fluctuate	(flŭk'tū āt)	To be undecided; to waver; to rise and fall, as in the case of prices on the stock market.
manifest(*v.*)	(măn'ĭ fĕst)	To make clear; to prove.
hostility	(hŏs tĭl'ĭ tĭ)	State of being opposed to something; antagonism; enmity.
infirm	(ĭn fûrm')	Feeble in body or health; shaky.

Cautions

Placate may be pronounced plā'kāt or plăk'āt.

Genial has a primary and a secondary pronunciation—
(1) jē'ni al; and (2) jēn'yal.

Miscellaneous Words Illustrated

1. My statement **pertinent** to the outcome of the affair was **erroneous**.
2. He is a very **influential** man in our community.
3. The child's **plaint** was that he was cold.
4. Will you **redeem** the theater tickets, since I cannot use them?
5. He was a typical Santa Claus, **genial** and kind.
6. We are trying to **beautify** our yard with trees and shrubs.
7. Let us try to **condone** her faults.
8. His **behavior** was always marked by **generosity** and courtesy.
9. I have no **record** of your past service.
10. Mary was trying to **placate** her angry brother.
11. We held a **conference** on the matter, but reached no conclusion.
12. The business, I am sure, will **flourish** under your management.
13. John's **jovial** manner made him very popular.
14. I **conclude,** from what you say, that you are unwilling to help me.
15. The prices of household articles **fluctuate** from time to time.
16. These writings **manifest** great vigor of style.
17. His **hostility** has followed me to **infirm** old age.

Exercise 1

1. Write a sentence using **record** as a verb.
2. Is **relative** a synonym of **pertinent**?
3. How is the antonym **impertinent** frequently used?

Exercise 2

1. Give the noun-form and adjective-form of **redeem**.
2. Is **beatify** the same as **beautify**? Prove your answer.
3. Write sentences containing:

conclusive   conclusion   manifest (*adj.*)   manifestation

4. What difference in meaning exists between **hostile** and **inimical**?
5. Give the noun-form of:

influential   genial   jovial

6. Use in sentences:

jovial disposition   influential standing
manifest purpose   limitless generosity

TEST II

(This test embraces material found in Lessons 14–28 inclusive.)

I. Construct sentences containing the following words:

exorbitant	reasonable	inestimable
litigant	validity	incriminate
amenable	solvent	stringency

II. Give the noun-form for each of these:

redeemable	consolidate	prosecute
illegal	influential	litigate

III. Write the verb-forms for:

violation	oppression	allegation
capitalist	testimony	negotiable

IV. Pronounce:

epitome	pecuniary	combatant
amenable	admirable	precedent
heinous	despicable	primarily

V. Use these expressions in sentences:

customary procedure	wave of prosperity
attendant circumstances	defer action
lucrative business	accurate appraisal

VI. Fill each blank below with the correct form of a word taken from this list:

accuracy	indicative	dissolving
inherit	exemption	testify

1. Conditions seemed to _____ a prosperous future.
2. We found it necessary to _____ the partnership.
3. The president of the firm demanded an _____ report.
4. The judge refused to consider Smith's _____.
5. Has Mr. Brophy paid his _____ tax?
6. In some states military men are _____ from paying the personal, or poll, tax.

LEGAL TERMS

clemency	(klĕm′ĕn sĭ)	Tendency to show mercy; compassion; leniency.
absolve	(ăb sŏlv′)	To release, as from an obligation; to clear of crime or guilt; acquit.
subpoena (*n.*)	(sŭb pē′nà)	An order to appear at court under a penalty for failure to do so.
expiate	(ĕks′pĭ āt)	To atone for.
ordinance	(ôr′dĭ năns)	An established law or statute.
relinquish	(rĕ lĭn′kwĭsh)	To abandon; leave; give up.
contributory	(kŏn trĭb′ů tô rĭ)	Giving or lending aid; tending to produce a result.
impair	(ĭm pâr′)	To reduce in quality, value, or otherwise; to damage, as in health, reputation, or fortune.
disinherit	(dĭs ĭn hĕr′ĭt)	To deprive or cut off someone, such as an heir, from property.
residue	(rĕz′ĭ dū)	That part of the estate left after all bills, bequests, and the like, are paid.
proceedings		The course of action in a law case.
misdemeanor	(—mēn′ẽr)	Ill-conduct; an offense less than a felony.
circumstantial	(—stăn′shăl)	Pertaining to circumstances; based on apparent facts.
alias	(ā′lĭ ăs)	An assumed name; a second writ, issued after a former one has expired.
abeyance	(ă bā′ăns)	A holding back for a time; temporary suspense.
domicile	(dŏm′ĭ sĭl)	Permanent place of abode; home.
default	(dĕ fôlt′)	Neglect; failure to perform something required by law.
aforesaid	(ă fôr′sĕd)	Said, or spoken of, before.

Caution

Note carefully that **alias** is pronounced **ā′lias,** and not **alī′as.**

Lesson 30

EXERCISES ON THE USE OF LEGAL TERMS

Match the words in Group I with their correct meanings, which are to be found in Group II, but not necessarily under the same numbers.

Group I

1. **surrogate** (sûr'rŏ găt)
2. **decedent** (dĕ sē'dĕnt)
3. **verbal** (vĕr'băl)
4. **institute** (ĭn'stĭ tūt)

5. **accessory** (ăk sĕs'sŏ rĭ)
6. **solicitor** (sŏ lĭs'ĭ tēr)
7. **technicality** (tĕk nĭ kăl'ĭ tĭ)
8. **executrix** (ĕg zĕk'ŭ trĭks)

Group II

1. To begin, to bring.
2. An accomplice.
3. The law officer of a city.
4. A female executor.

5. Expressed in spoken words.
6. A deceased person.
7. A judicial officer with jurisdiction over the probate of wills.

8. A term or expression peculiar to any trade, profession, or art.

True or False Test

Which of the following statements are true and which are false? Are there any misused words?

1. An **appellant** is one who takes an appeal from a judicial decree.
2. A written declaration that is not taken under oath is called an **affidavit**.
3. If Mr. Smith killed a person, he would be charged with **homicide**.
4. The person who gives a mortgage is called a **mortgagee**.
5. To **catechize** means to **question** or to **interrogate**.
6. An **invalid** claim is one that is not recognized by law.
7. **Lenient** may be pronounced either *lēn'i ent* or *lēn'yent*.
8. Mr. Pronovost **councilled** his pupils against wasting their time while in school.
9. The letter **i** in **requital** is pronounced like the **i** in **acquittal**.
10. The counsel for the state is called a **persecuting attorney**.
11. **Repeal** may be used as a noun or as a verb.

42

Lesson 31

LEGAL TERMS

executor	(ĕg zĕk′ û tēr)	A doer or performer; a man appointed to carry out the provisions of a will.
jurisdiction	(jū rĭs dĭk′shŭn)	Right or power to execute judicial authority.
negligence	(nĕg′lĭ jĕns)	Disregard of duty; carelessness.
litigation	(lĭt ĭ gā′shŭn)	Process of trial at law.
codicil	(kŏd′ĭ sĭl)	A legal addition to a will, modifying it in some respect.
larceny	(lär′sĕ nĭ)	Unlawful taking of another's personal property without that one's consent.
forgery	(fōr′jĕr ĭ)	Act of producing falsely or changing a writing, such as a signature, with intention to defraud.
malfeasance	(măl fē′zăns)	Official misconduct.
homicide	(hŏm′ĭ sīd)	The killing of one human being by another.
annulment	(ă nŭl′mĕnt)	Act of abolishing or making void.
mandamus	(măn dā′mŭs)	The writ issued to enforce performance of a public duty.
invalid	(ĭn văl′ĭd)	Of no force or binding effect; void.
falsify	(fôl′sĭ fī)	To represent falsely; to change wrongly.
adjudged	(ă jŭjd′)	Decided judicially.
waiver	(wāv′ēr)	Act of relinquishing something, such as a right.
legacy	(lĕg′à sĭ)	A gift of property by will.
injunction	(ĭn jŭnk′shŭn)	A court order, usually restraining from some act.
bequeath	(bĕ kwēth′)	To give or leave by will.
indictment	(ĭn dīt′mĕnt)	Formal written statement of an offense.
administer	(ăd mĭn′ĭs tēr)	To settle something, such as an estate; to manage.
judicial	(joō dĭsh′ăl)	Pertaining to the administration of justice.
inquest	(ĭn′kwĕst)	Judicial inquiry before a jury, usually into the causes of a death.

Legal Terms Illustrated

The preceding legal terms are here illustrated in sentences:

1. Mr. Lowe was appointed **executor** of the will.
2. This district is not under your **jurisdiction.**
3. The driver was accused of **negligence.**
4. The question is now in **litigation.**
5. According to the terms of the **codicil,** his share was reduced.
6. The charge against this man is **larceny.**
7. The **forgery** of the name was not noticed for some time.
8. The **malfeasance** was a shock to the public.
9. The prisoner was freed of the charge of **homicide.**
10. The **annulment** of this law was approved by all.
11. A **mandamus** was issued to force the mayor to act.
12. The trial was declared **invalid.**
13. The witness attempted to **falsify.**
14. It is impossible to **adjudge** the matter until both sides are heard.
15. A **waiver** of this point was made by the defense.
16. A large **legacy** was left to Mr. Lacey.
17. An **injunction** forbidding the opening of the house was granted.
18. Mrs. Adams did not **bequeath** her fortune to her son.
19. The **indictment,** as brought in by the grand jury, was serious.
20. Mr. Jones was appointed to **administer** the estate.
21. The **judicial** proceedings attracted a large number.
22. The coroner's **inquest** indicated that the man committed suicide.

Exercise

1. Give five words of the **teneo-** or **tain-**family, such as retained.

2. What two Latin words form the word **jurisdiction?**

3. Give the meaning of:

   judicious   judiciary   **jurisprudence**

4. Name two synonyms for **irrelevant.**

Questions

1. Is there any difference in meaning between **indictment** and **inditement?**

2. If you change the accent of **invalid** to the first syllable, how is the meaning affected?

Lesson 32

MULTIPLE-CHOICE EXERCISE

Which of the two words enclosed in parentheses is correct? Most of these words have already been studied.

1. To sell opium is (**illegal, eligible**).
2. My brother was held (**culpable, neglectful**) of the theft.
3. The (**allegation, rebuttal**) was that Brown entered the building without permission.
4. Many persons are convicted on (**circumstantial, artificial**) evidence.
5. The millionaire disinherited his son on account of his many (**misdemeanors, demeanors**).
6. The court has no (**jurisprudence, jurisdiction**) over this personal affair of mine.
7. The prisoner was (**resolved, absolved**) from all blame.
8. To write the name of another person on a check and cash it is (**larceny, forgery**).
9. The boy paid no attention to the (**counsel, council**) offered him by his lawyer.
10. The person who commences a legal action or suit is called the (**defendant, plaintiff**).
11. The attorney asked that the prisoner be (**prosecuted, persecuted**) to the full extent of the law.
12. It was agreed that no (**irreverent, irrelevant**) testimony would be accepted.
13. A synonym for **appraisal** is (**praise, estimate**).
14. It was difficult to have the man (**ascent, assent**) to the accusation that he stole the purse.
15. The legal inquiry into the cause of a sudden death is called an (**inquest, bequest**).

Questions

1. What do we call **ir-** in **irrelevant**, **il-** in **illegal**, **in-** in **inquest**, and **circum-** in **circumstantial**?

2. Use **counsel** as a verb.

3. From what verb is **allegation** derived?

4. If **culpable** means deserving of blame or censure, what does **exculpate** mean?

45

WORDS OF THE 4,000 POSITION IN THORNDIKE'S LIST

renounce	To disown; to cast off; to give up.
vicious	Corrupt; wicked; immoral.
restraint	The act of holding back or hindering from action.
reduction	A lessening in quantity or numbers; simplification in form.
security	Safety; state of being protected; pledge or guarantee of performance.
medical	Pertaining to the treatment of disease.
picturesque	Suitable to be drawn or painted as a picture.
temperance	Moderation; habit of avoiding extremes.
overwhelm	To flow over something completely; to over-power; to swallow up, as in the case of a flood.
guiltless	Without crime or wickedness.
inheritance	A gift or bequest received from an ancestor or other person.
persecute	To pursue in order to injure or afflict.
precept	A rule of action or of moral conduct.
stature	Height; tallness.
righteous	Blameless; virtuous; upright.
fragrance	A sweet odor.
implore	To entreat earnestly; to beg or pray.
extract (*v.*) (—trăkt')	To draw or obtain from; to pull out of.
cherish	To hold dear; to treat with tenderness.
dedicate	To devote to some cause; to set apart for some purpose.

Exercise

Use in sentences:

cherished hopes   righteous indignation
guiltless conscience   feeling of security
radical reduction   medical attention

Words Illustrated

The words in the preceding list are here illustrated in sentences:

1. The king **renounced** the throne in favor of his son.
2. The **vicious** act was the work of an insane person.
3. He placed no **restraint** upon his temper.
4. There is a general **reduction** in prices.
5. There was no **security** against the animals of the forest.
6. This man requires **medical** attention.
7. The view of the lake and mountains was very **picturesque.**
8. Mr. Baker was made head of the **Temperance** League.
9. Mr. Nolan won the presidency by an **overwhelming** majority.
10. The prisoner was pronounced **guiltless.**
11. He received a vast **inheritance** from his father.
12. Mrs. Brown's enemies continued to **persecute** her.
13. A **precept** of our organization is brotherly love.
14. Everett was a man of great **stature,** measuring six feet, four inches when he was twenty-one years of age.
15. The people rose in **righteous** indignation against the injustice of the act.
16. There was always the **fragrance** of flowers in the room.
17. Although we **implored** him to stay, he paid no attention to our entreaty.
18. The young man resolved to **extract** as much joy from life as possible.
19. The country will always **cherish** the memory of the brave men who died in the war.
20. The President spoke when the Tomb of the Unknown Soldier was **dedicated** as a national memorial.

Exercise

Construct sentences containing the following words:

inherit
reduce
restrain
resolution
extraction

organize
renunciation
imploration
dedicatory —
overwhelm

47

Lesson 34

MEDICAL TERMS

cerebral (sĕr'—) Pertaining to the brain.

tubercular (tŭ bĕr'kŭ lȧr) Affected with consumption.

atrophy (*n.*) (ăt'rŏ fĭ) A wasting away, or lack of growth, from want of nourishment.

cardiac (kär'—) Pertaining to the heart.

tetanus (tĕt'—) An acute disease, sometimes known as "lockjaw," causing muscular rigidity.

pulmonary (pŭl'—) Pertaining to the lungs.

paresis (pȧ rē'sĭs; pär'ĕ sĭs) Incomplete paralysis, affecting movement but not feeling.

delirium (—lĭr'—) A temporary state of mental disturbance, marked by disordered speech and other symptoms.

incision (ĭn sĭzh'—) A cut made by a sharp instrument.

abdominal (ăb dŏm'—) Pertaining to the abdomen.

stethoscope (stĕth'—) An instrument designed to convey to the ear the sounds of the heart and of other organs.

cuticle (kū'tĭ k'l) A skin or membrane.

amputate (ăm'—) To cut off (a limb or portion of a limb).

vertebra (vûr'—) One of the bones of the spinal column.

antitoxin (—tŏk'sĭn) A substance introduced into the blood to prevent or cure illness by neutralizing the poison made by a disease-causing germ.

alienist (āl'yĕn ĭst) One who specializes in the treatment of mental diseases.

dissect (dĭ sĕkt') To divide a body or object into separate parts for examination.

narcotic (—kŏt'—) A drug, such as opium, which relieves pain and produces sleep.

serum (sē'—) Watery fluid left after the rest of a sample of the blood has been removed by artificial process.

diphtheria (dĭf thē'—) An acute, infectious disease in which the air passages, especially the throat, become coated with a false membrane.

48

MEDICAL TERMS

hemorrhage	(hĕm'ŏ rǎj)	Profuse escape of blood from a blood vessel; excessive bleeding.
glycerine	(glĭs'ẽr ĭn)	A colorless liquid with a sweetish taste, obtained from natural fats and oils.
infection	(ĭn fĕk'shŭn)	The communication of disease germs.
jugular	(jŭg'ů lẽr; jōō'gů lẽr)	Pertaining to the neck or throat.
asthma	(ăz'mȧ)	A disease of the throat and bronchial passages attended by coughing and heavy breathing.
diagnosis	(dī ăg nō'sĭs)	Any explanation based on an examination of facts.
mercurochrome	(mẽr kūr'ŏ krōm)	An antiseptic, often used as a substitute for iodine in the dressing of wounds.
prophylactic	(prō fĭ lăk'tĭk)	A medicine that prevents or protects from disease.
hiccough	(hĭk'ŭp)	A short, gasping sound made by a quick, involuntary inhalation of breath.
nausea	(nô'shĕ ȧ)	Sickness of the stomach, such as seasickness.
hygiene	(hī'jēn; hī'jĭ ēn)	The science which treats of the preservation of health and the prevention of disease.
unconscious	(ŭn kŏn'shŭs)	Not mentally awake; without apparent feeling or sensation.
rheumatic	(rōō măt'ĭk)	Pertaining to rheumatism.
liniment	(lĭn'ĭ mĕnt)	A liquid applied to the skin to soothe or stimulate.
arsenic	(är'sĕn ĭk)	A solid chemical element, found in white crystals; poisonous compound with oxygen.
alimentary	(ăl ĭ mĕn'tȧ rĭ)	Pertaining to food or nutrition.

Lesson 36

MISCELLANEOUS WORDS

appropriate (*adj.*)	(ăp prō′prĭ ăt)	Suitable; proper.
demeanor	(dě mēn′ẽr)	Conduct; deportment.
demolish	(dě mŏl′ĭsh)	To destroy; ruin.
artificial	(är tĭ fĭ′shål)	Not natural; mechanical.
delinquent (*n.*)	(dě lĭn′kwĕnt)	One who neglects a duty; offender.
ruffian	(rŭf′fĭ ăn)	An unruly person.
ludicrous	(lū′dĭ krŭs)	Producing ridicule or laughter.
erroneous	(ĕr rō′nĕ ŭs)	Misleading; false; untrue.
certainty	(sẽr′tĭn tĭ)	State of being sure or definite.
duplicity	(dů plĭs′ĭ tĭ)	Double-dealing; deceit.
suspicious	(sŭs pĭ′shŭs)	Distrustful; questionable.
arbitrator	(är′bĭ trā tẽr)	One who has power to decide.
extricate	(ĕks′trĭ kāt)	To free from difficulties.
ultimately	(ŭl′tĭ măt lĭ)	Finally; in the end.
recuperate	(rě kū′pẽr āt)	To recover; get well.
superfluous	(sů pẽr′floo ŭs)	Not necessary; excessive.

Some of the words given above are here used in sentences:

1. We have great **certainty** that our side will **ultimately** win.
2. His remarks upon the subject were both **ludicrous** and **superfluous.**
3. The **delinquent** tried to **extricate** himself from the meshes of the law.
4. The rumor that the king was **recuperating** was **erroneous.**
5. There will be **appropriate** exercises in the school on Washington's Birthday.
6. The buildings were **demolished** by the enemy's guns.
7. The man has an **artificial** arm.
8. The **ruffian** was ejected from the theater by the policeman.

True or False Test

Which statements are false?

1. **Duplicity** is commonly used in a bad sense.
2. **Ruffian** is never pronounced ruf′fan.
3. **Misdemeanor** is an antonym for **demeanor.**
4. **Delinquent** has only a noun form.

MEDICAL TERMS

pestilence	(pĕs′—)	Any contagious or infectious disease that is widespread and fatal.
symptom	(sĭmp′—)	Any affection accompanying a disease; a sign; an indication.
tendency	(tĕn′—)	Inclination or likelihood to take some course.
dyspeptic (n.)	(dĭs pĕp′—)	A person having dyspepsia, or indigestion.
germicidal	(—sīd′—)	Destructive to germs.
anodyne	(ăn′ṓ dīn)	A remedy serving to soothe pain.
infirmary	(ĭn fûr′—)	A hospital or other place for the infirm or sick.
abscess	(ăb′sĕs)	A collection of pus, owing to injury or poisoning.
ataxia	(ȧ tăk′sĭ ȧ)	Lack of power to co-ordinate voluntary muscular movements.
malady	(măl′—)	Any disease of the human body.
eczema	(ĕk′zĕ mȧ)	An inflammatory itching of the skin.
antiseptic (adj.)	(—sĕpt′—)	Tending to prevent pus formation by destroying the growth of bacteria.
incipient	(—sĭp′—)	Beginning to appear.
vitality	(vī tăl′—)	Life force; capacity for resisting disease and the approach of old age.
post-mortem	(—môrt′—)	Made after death.
disinfect	(—fĕkt′)	To free from infection or its possibility.
chiropodist	(kī rŏp′—)	One who treats diseases of the feet and hands.
opiate (n.)	(ṓ′pĭ ȧt)	Any narcotic medicine containing opium.
dilute	(dĭ lūt′)	To make thinner; to weaken.

Caution

Note well the pronunciation of **eczema**. It is **ĕk′zĕ mȧ**, not **ĕk zē′mȧ**.

MEDICAL TERMS

tuberculosis (tŭ bēr kŭ lō'sĭs) A wasting disease usually affecting the lungs, often called "consumption."

peritonitis (pĕr ĭ tŏ nī'tĭs) Acute inflammation of the membrane lining the abdomen.

quinine (kwī'nīn; kwĭ nēn') A bitter drug made from the bark of the cinchona tree, used in medicine for treating fevers and other ailments.

inoculate (ĭn ŏk'ů lāt) To infect with a disease by inserting its poison in the flesh.

disinfectant (dĭs ĭn fĕkt'ănt) A preparation that will destroy germs.

chloroform (klō'rŏ fôrm) A colorless liquid, the vapor of which produces insensibility.

denature (dĕ nā'tůr) To render unfit for eating or drinking without impairing.

curative (kūr'ă tĭv) Relating to the cure of a disease.

stimulant (stĭm'ů lănt) Something tending to produce a temporary increase of vitality.

antidote (ăn'tĭ dōt) A remedy to counteract the effects of poison.

epilepsy (ĕp'ĭ lĕp sĭ) A disease attended by sudden loss of consciousness and convulsive muscular movements.

phlegm (flĕm) Thick mucus discharged from the throat.

malignant (mă lĭg'nănt) Tending to produce death.

cauterize (kô'tēr īz) To burn or sear with a hot iron or some caustic agent.

sterilize (stĕr'ĭ līz) To destroy germs or bacteria by the use of a heat or chemical.

perspiratory (pēr spīr'ă tŏ rĭ) Pertaining to perspiration.

neuritis (nů rī'tĭs) Inflammation of a nerve or nerves.

caffeine (kăf'ĕ ĭn; kăf'ēn) A stimulant found in coffee, tea, and certain other drinks.

TEST III

(This test embraces material found in Lessons 29–38, inclusive.)

I. Write a word related to each of the following words:

amputate	solicitor	litigation
alienist	negligence	annulment
incipient	vitality	inoculate

II. What is the correct pronunciation of each word?

eczema	diphtheria	indictment
phlegm	alienist	dedicatory
atrophy	jugular	preferable

III. Find in Group 2 the definitions for the words in Group 1, indicating them by number:

Group 1

1. sterilize
2. dissect
3. irrelevant
4. abeyance
5. precept
6. cauterize
7. sustain
8. cherish

Group 2

1. A rule.
2. To burn with a hot iron.
3. To hold dear.
4. To uphold or support.
5. Not applicable.
6. To destroy germs by heat or otherwise.
7. Temporary suspense.
8. To divide into parts.

IV. Give the preferred pronunciation of:

hygiene	paresis	strychnine
dilute	caffeine	quinine

V. Construct sentences containing:

contributory factor	invalid excuse
erroneous rumor	malignant disease
dedicatory exercises	repulsive sight

53

Lesson 39

WORDS FROM THE AYRE-BUCKINGHAM SCALE

The per cent at the top of each column of words indicates the percentage of correct spellings that a freshman class should average on these words without having made any preparation.

84%	79%	73%
emergency	convenient	accuracy
appreciate	preliminary	digestible
sincerely	disappoint	principle
athletic	committee	decision
practical	associates	seized
cordially	beneficial	precipice
vicinity	especially	surgeon
sensible	immediate	mucilage
nonsense	exquisite	restaurant
calendar	treachery	parliament
disease	financier	resemblance
antique	opportunity	accommodate
separate	intelligent	millionaire
character	architecture	counterfeit
organization	confectionery	thoroughly
consequence	development	superintendent

Cautions

Particular attention should be given to the following facts:

Cordially is pronounced kôr′jăl lĭ.

Athletic has three syllables and is never pronounced ăth-thē lĕt′ĭc.

Principle (*n.*) is often confused with **principal** (*adj.* or *n.*).

Exercise

How many mistakes in spelling are there in these two sentences?

1. A confectionary store does not always have digestible merchandise.
2. The superintendant was very accommodating.

Lesson 40

WORDS OF THE 6,000–7,000 POSITION IN THORNDIKE'S LIST

beautify	(bū′tĭ fī)	To adorn; to make charming.
fortitude	(fôr′tĭ tūd)	Mental strength to endure suffering.
broach (*v.*)	(brōch)	To begin a discussion about.
arrogant	(ăr′ŏ gănt)	Overestimating his own importance; haughty.
catastrophe	(kȧ tăs′trŏ fĕ)	Sudden calamity; disaster.
integrity	(ĭn tĕg′rĭ tĭ)	Honesty; uprightness.
malicious	(mȧ lĭsh′ŭs)	Influenced by hatred or spite.
oblivion	(ŏb lĭv′ĭ ŭn)	Forgetfulness; lack of memory.
clamorous	(klăm′ēr ŭs)	Noisy; riotous.
mischievous	(mĭs′chĭ vŭs)	Hurtful; causing annoyance; impish.
surmount	(sûr mount′)	To rise above; overcome.
intellectual	(ĭn tĕ lĕkt′û ăl)	Pertaining to the mind; mental.
notorious	(nŏ tō′rĭ ŭs)	Publicly known (in a bad sense).
propitious	(prŏ pĭsh′ ŭs)	Favorably inclined; fortunate.
frantic	(frăn′tĭk)	Violently mad; wild; disorderly.
obscurity	(ŏb skū′rĭ tĭ)	Lack of clearness or prominence; indistinctness.

Note well that **mischievous** has two, and not three, **i's.**

Exercise 1

1. Construct sentences containing:

beautify	oblivion	mischievous

2. Write a sentence containing: the adjectival form of **surmount**; the adverbial form of **obscurity**; the noun-form of **arrogant**.

3. To which of the words listed above are these related?

clamor	oblivious	propitiate
malice	notoriety	intelligence
mischief	intellect	arrogance

55

Words Illustrated

The following sentences show uses of some words given in the preceding list:

1. Spring was just beginning to **beautify** the landscape.
2. Her **fortitude** in sorrow was an example to all.
3. At this unfavorable time I did not wish to **broach** the subject.
4. Although his position was an enviable one, there was nothing **arrogant** about him.
5. The burning of so many houses was a dreadful **catastrophe.**
6. The **integrity** of his character was never doubted.
7. There was nothing **malicious** about the child.
8. His mind was confused; his act of yesterday was in **oblivion.**
9. There was a **clamorous** denial from all.
10. The little spaniel was spirited and **mischievous.**
11. He was able to **surmount** great difficulties.
12. The conversation was interesting and **intellectual.**
13. The city was becoming **notorious** for its crime.
14. The weather was not **propitious** for football.
15. The **obscurity** of the house caused some of the visitors to go astray.
16. I made a **frantic** effort to catch the vase before it fell.

Exercise 2

A. How does **notoriety** differ from **publicity?**

B. Select the proper word:

1. A hermit lives in (**splendor, poverty, obscurity**).
2. The president seemed to be (**neglectful, active, oblivious**) of the fact that it was his birthday.
3. (**Arrogance, notoriety, integrity**) in a man is essential to success.
4. We were unable to (**orate, listen, broach**) the subject to our president.
5. One must (**amount, relinquish, surmount**) many obstacles before he is successful.
6. The poor woman showed great (**fortitude, ability, integrity**) while in trouble.

REAL ESTATE TERMS

mortgage (môr′găj) A giving over of property as security for the payment of a debt.

foreclose (fôr klōz′) To take away another's right to redeem his mortgaged property, following non-payment of debt.

probate (*n.*) (prō′bāt) Official proof, especially of a legal instrument offered, such as the last will and testament of a person deceased.

depreciate (dĕ prē′shĭ āt) To lessen in price or estimated value.

encumbrance (ĕn kŭm′brăns) That which burdens; a lien attached to real property.

occupancy (ŏk′ŭ păn sĭ) The act of dwelling in, or of taking and holding in possession, something, such as a house.

quitclaim (kwĭt′klām) A full release, as from a demand, suit, or other obligation.

tenant (tĕn′ănt) One who by agreement lives in or holds possession of real estate owned by another.

premises (prĕm′ĭ sĕs) Real estate; a building or a piece of land.

lessee (lĕs ē′) A tenant who has a lease.

trespass (trĕs′pås) To enter unlawfully upon the property of another.

estate (ĕs tāt′) Property, in general.

liquidate (lĭk′wĭ dāt) To pay off something, such as a debt; to arrange or settle something, such as the affairs of a bankrupt.

receivership (rĕ sēv′ĕr shĭp) Office of one who holds in trust property under litigation.

permanent (pûr′må nĕnt) Continuing in the same state, or without any change that destroys form or character.

amortize (a môr′tīz) To set aside money regularly in a fund for future payment of (a debt, etc.).

Lesson 42

MISCELLANEOUS WORDS WITH COMPLETION EXERCISE

ratify	(răt'ĭ fī)	Formally to approve of; to indorse.
severity	(sĕ vĕr'ĭ tĭ)	Harshness; strictness.
humility	(hû mĭl'ĭ tĭ)	Modesty; self-abasement.
grievance	(grēv'ăns)	Sense of wrong; just complaint.
servitude	(sûr'vĭ tūd)	Slavery; bondage; enforced labor.
illumine	(ĭ lū'mĭn)	To light up; to shine upon.
malicious	(mă lĭsh'ŭs)	Influenced by hatred or spite.
impetuous	(ĭm pĕt'û ŭs)	Rushing with force; hasty in action.

Exercise 1

Fill each blank with an appropriate word taken from the preceding list:

1. One of the preacher's outstanding qualities was his _____.
2. The Senate refused to _____ the treaty.
3. The Magna Carta did not free persons held in penal _____ by the state.
4. The new lights greatly _____ the boulevard.
5. The _____ remarks made by the adversaries of the President were uncalled for.
6. We could not accomplish much good with the _____ youth.
7. The _____ of Nero's rule will be criticized forever by historians.
8. The young athlete refused to take part in any more games because of a _____ he had against the coach.

Exercise 2

1. What is the adjective related to **severity?**
2. Make sentences containing:
   humble   grieve   ratification
3. Give a synonym for:
   humility   malicious   servitude
4. Use in a sentence the noun-form of:
   grieve   impetuous   illumine

58

Lesson 43

INSURANCE TERMS

policy	(pŏl'ĭ sĭ)	A document containing a contract of insurance.
beneficiary	(bĕn ĕ físh'ĭ ā'rĭ)	One who receives the proceeds of a will or an insurance policy.
premium	(prē'mĭ ŭm)	The rate paid for insurance.
indemnity	(ĭn dĕm'nĭ tĭ)	Repayment for loss.
expire	(ĕks pīr')	To come to an end.
annuity	(ă nū'ĭ tĭ)	A certain amount paid yearly.
cancel	(kăn'sĕl)	To annul; revoke.
reimburse	(rē ĭm bûrs')	To pay back; refund.
mortality	(môr tăl'ĭ tĭ)	Number of deaths in proportion to population.
mutual	(mū'tŭ ăl)	Relating to a company in which the policyholders receive dividends.
dividends	(dĭv'ĭ dĕndz)	The profits of the company paid to policyholders.
lapse	(lăps)	To end (said of a claim) through failure to observe its terms.
arson	(är'sŏn)	The intentional setting fire to, and burning of, any building.
hazardous	(hăz'ăr dŭs)	Risky; dangerous.
endowment	(ĕn dŏw'mĕnt)	A form of insurance in which a lump sum is paid to the beneficiary at the end of a certain period.
actuary	(ăk'tŭ ă rĭ)	One skilled in computing life insurance, risks, premiums, and the like.
underwriter	(ŭn'dĕr rīt ĕr)	One who has an insurance business.

Some of these words are here used in sentences:

1. What **premium** do you pay on your life insurance?
2. The Metropolitan Life Insurance Company pays **dividends** and is, therefore, a **mutual** organization.
3. He let his insurance **lapse** two years ago.
4. I was **reimbursed** during my illness by the insurance company.
5. When does your **endowment** policy **expire**?
6. People with **hazardous** positions, such as aviators and steeplejacks, find it difficult to procure insurance.

59

MISCELLANEOUS WORDS WITH COMPLETION EXERCISE

memorize	(mĕm′ō rīz)	To learn by heart.
receptacle	(rĕ sĕp′tȧ k′l)	That which serves to receive or contain something.
fascinate	(făs′ĭ nāt)	To charm.
hypocrisy	(hĭ pŏk′rĭ sĭ)	Act of feigning to be what one is not.
abridge	(ȧ brĭj′)	To shorten.
ravenous	(răv′ĕn ŭs)	Furiously hungry.
misuse (n.)	(mĭs ūs′)	Wrong use; abuse.
calculate	(kăl′ků lāt)	To reckon.
facility	(fȧ sĭl′ĭ tĭ)	Lack of difficulty; that which disposes toward readiness in accomplishment.
abject	(ăb′jĕkt)	Sunk to a low condition.
combatant	(kŏm′bȧt ănt)	One who contends or fights.
intrude	(ĭn trōōd′)	To force in or on.
firmness	(fûrm′nĕss)	State of being fixed or unyielding.
malady	(măl′ȧ dĭ)	Any disease of the human body; a disorder; a defect.
advocate (v.)	(ăd′vō kāt)	To plead in favor of.
recognition	(rĕk ŏg nĭ′shŭn)	Act of acknowledging; identification on a second meeting.

Exercise

Fill the blanks with words from the preceding list.

1. That man is a _____ eater.
2. The family soon found itself in _____ misery.
3. There is a great _____ of the words **affect** and **effect.**
4. One of the _____ received a severe injury during the fight.
5. Every _____ to improve oneself can be found in our schools.
6. Do you _____ daylight saving time?
7. The visitor failed to receive any _____ from the President.

Lesson 45

GEOGRAPHIC NAMES

United States

Gloucester	(glŏs'tẽr)	Wichita	(wĭch'ĭ tô)
Barre	(băr'ĕ)	Arkansas	(är'kăn sô)
Cayuga	(kă yōō'gä)	Raleigh	(rô'lĭ)
Oneida	(ŏ nī'dä)	Macon	(mā'kŏn)
Genesee	(jĕn ĕ sē')	Natchez	(năch'ĕz)
Schenectady	(skĕ nĕk'tă dĭ)	Houston	(hūs'tŭn)
Reading	(rĕd'ĭng)	Cheyenne	(shī ĕn')
Illinois	(ĭl ĭ noi')	Pueblo	(pwĕb'lō)
Iowa	(ī'ô wä	Helena	(hĕl'ĕ nä)
Sioux	(sōō)	Boise	(boi'sĭ)
Joliet	(jō'lĭ ĕt)	Spokane	(spô kăn')
Sault Ste. Marie	(sōō' sănt mả rē')	San Jose	(săn hō sā')
Racine	(rả sēn')	Los Angeles	(lōs ăng'gĕl ĕs;
Palo Alto	(pä'lō äl'tō)		lŏs ăn'jĕl ēz)

Miami   (mī ăm'ĭ)

Canada

Quebec	(kwĕ bĕk')
Saguenay	(săg ē nā')
Regina	(rĕ jī'nä)
Sydney	(sĭd'nĭ)
Cobalt	(kō'bôlt)

Caution

Arkansas, the state, should not be called **Ar kan'sas.**

Questions

1. From what language are the following words taken?

     Sault Ste. Marie   Boise

2. How many Indian names can you find in the preceding list?

3. Give two other geographical names, ending like Gloucester in **ester,** which have silent letters.

4. Is **St. Helena** pronounced like **Helena?**

5. What is the sound of **a** in **Spokane?**

61

Lesson 46

TEXTILE AND FURNITURE TERMS

Can you tell to which of the two groups each of the following words belongs?

taboret	(tăb'ŏ rĕt)	adjustable	(ăd jŭs'tȧ b'l)
embroideries		bureau	(bū'rō)
damask	(dăm'—)	cashmere	(kăsh'mēr)
ingrain		brocade	(brō kād')
buffet	(boŏ fā')	percale	(pĕr kāl')
cambric		broadcloth	(brôd'—)
worsted	(woŏs'tĕd)	pedestal	
crinoline	(—lǐn; —lēn)	settee	(sĕ tē')
remnants		wicker	
antique	(—tēk')	fumed	(fūmd)
chiffonier	(shǐ fŏn ēr')	rattan	(ră tăn')
lacquer	(lăk'ēr)	veneer	(vĕ nēr')
upholstered		warp	
cheviot	(shĕv'ǐ ŏt)	denim	(dĕn'ǐm)
taffeta	(tăf'—)	seasoned	
pongee	(—jē')	mercerize	(—īz)
chiffon	(shǐf'on; shǐ fŏn')	crochet	(krō shā')
weathered		tapestry	(tăp'ĕs trǐ)
renovate		organdie	(ôr'găn dǐ)
alpaca	(ăl păk'ȧ)	suite	(swēt)
divan	(dī'văn; dǐ văn')	tatting	(tăt'—)
sateen	(să tēn')	inlaid	
davenport	(dăv'ĕn pôrt)	commode	(kŏ mōd')
luster		linoleum	(lǐ nō'—)

Exercise

1. Has **buffet** another pronunciation?

2. Explain the use of **veneer** in:

He possesses only a **veneer** of culture.

3. Use in sentences: **weathered, seasoned, taboret.**

4. Give the meaning of the bold-type words:

a. The leg of that chair must be **renovated.**

b. The seats and desks in the classroom are **adjustable.**

c. Should one ever apply **lacquer** to a **bureau?**

Lesson 47

WORDS ILLUSTRATED

Can you derive the meaning of each of the bold-type words by its use in the sentence? These words occupy the 5,500–6,000 position in Thorndike's List.

suspicious	We were always **suspicious** of Jones on account of his past record.
preference	Many pupils show a **preference** for French rather than Latin.
gnash	Whenever the man was really angry, he would **gnash** his teeth.
fraternal	The Elks is one of the largest **fraternal** organizations in this country.
co-operate	In the ideal high school the pupils **co-operate** with the principal toward the upkeep of the school.
absolve	The jury **absolved** the prisoner from all blame of the murder.
hospitality	The Southern people were always **hospitable** to strangers.
contemplate	The Board of Education does not **contemplate** building another high school.
approval	The boy, having received the **approval** of his parents, joined the navy.
tempestuous	Our ship was nearly wrecked by the **tempestuous** sea.
concede	The defeated candidate for the mayoralty refused to **concede** the election until a recount of votes had been made.
agitate	The city was much **agitated**, owing to the threatened strike of the trolley-men.
wayward	The judge decided to send the **wayward** boy to a reform school.
strenuous	The basket-ball team made a **strenuous** effort to overcome the opponents' lead.
adversity	In time of **adversity** one should endeavor to look upon the bright side of life.

Preference is pronounced *prĕf'ẽr ĕns*.
Contemplate has two pronunciations.

Lesson 48

MISCELLANEOUS WORDS WITH EXERCISE

hostility		Unfriendliness; opposition.
guidance		Direction; leading; supervision.
insurgent		One who rises against authority.
palpable	(păl′—)	Capable of being touched or felt; easily seen.
pacify	(păs′—)	To calm or appease; to restore to quiet.
humiliate		To put to shame; to humble.
legislate	(lĕj′—)	To make, or enact, a law or laws.
intricate		Involved; complicated.
hereditary		Transmitted from parent to child.
infallible		Incapable of erring; unfailing.
ambiguous	(—bĭg′—)	Doubtful; having two or more possible meanings.
deformity		That which disfigures, or spoils the shape of, some person or thing.
habitual		Customary; fixed by repetition.
pitiable		Deserving of sympathy.
advisable		In accordance with good judgment.
intervene	(—vēn′)	To come, or be situated, between.

Exercise 1

1. Give the noun-forms for:

advisable   ambiguous   habitual   pitiable

2. How do the prefixes in these words affect their meanings?

intervene   deformity   infallible

3. How do the suffixes affect these words?

advisable   guidance   pitiable

4. Use in sentences:

palpable wrong   insurgent group
intricate problem   ambiguous statement

Words Illustrated

The preceding list of words is here illustrated in sentences:

1. There was no **hostility** existing between his family and mine.
2. Under the **guidance** of Miss Carewe, the child made rapid progress.
3. There was one member of the staff who was regarded as an **insurgent.**
4. It was not a **palpable** error and, therefore, was overlooked.
5. We did everything to **pacify** the unfortunate girl, but were unsuccessful.
6. His guilt did not **humiliate** him.
7. Whether or not they will **legislate** the bill at this session is a question.
8. He was fond of solving **intricate** problems.
9. The boy's generosity was **hereditary.**
10. As a weather prophet, he was not **infallible.**
11. The terms of the speaker were **ambiguous,** and therefore not easily understood.
12. His **deformity** was no hindrance to fame and popularity.
13. Mr. Kay is an **habitual** smoker of strong cigars.
14. The child was a **pitiable** object after the accident.
15. We considered it **advisable** to postpone the meeting.
16. Two weeks will **intervene** between the lectures.

Exercise 2

1. Write a word that is related to each of these:

   hostility   pacify   intricacy

2. Construct sentences using these words:

   habitable   habitation   intervention

3. Consult your dictionary for the distinction between **pitiable** and **pitiful.**

4. Place the noun-form of **humiliate** in a sentence.

5. From what languages are **ambiguous, intervene,** and **legislate** derived?

6. **Fallacy, intricacy, pacifist,** and **legislation** are related to what words in the list above?

Lesson 49

WORDS OF THE 6,000–7,000 POSITION
IN THORNDIKE'S LIST

vibrate	(vī'—)	To throb, to tremble.
satiate	(sā'shĭ āt)	To satisfy the appetite or desire of.
validity		Quality of being sound, true, or sufficient.
nourish		To feed or support.
overwhelm		To overcome with emotion; to bury or drown.
verify	(věr'ĭ—)	To prove to be true.
notable	(nō'tȧ b'l)	Distinguished; worthy of attention.
secondary		Being of second place.
pensive		Dreamily or sadly thoughtful.
anguish	(ăng'gwĭsh)	Extreme pain of either body or mind.
defile	(dĕ fīl')	To make foul; to corrupt; to soil or blemish.
perilous		Dangerous; venturous.
utility		Quality of being useful.
affliction		Distress or suffering.
vacillate	(văs'ĭ lāt)	To waver; to be changeable.
sanction (v.)	(săngk'shŭn)	To approve; to confirm; to permit.

True or False Test

Are the following statements true or false?

1. **Hazardous** is an antonym of **perilous**.
2. The prefixes of **defile** and **affliction** are **de** and **af**.
3. The noun-form of **satiate** is **satiety**.
4. The adjectival form of **validity** is **valid**.
5. **Vac** in **vacillate** is pronounced as if it were spelled **fas**.
6. **Vibratory** is derived from **vibrate**.
7. **Sanction** may be used as a noun or a verb.

Exercise

1. What are the adjective-forms of these words?

   vibrate   **validity**   **nourish**

2. Give the antonym of **secondary**.

66

Words Illustrated

The words of the preceding list are here illustrated in sentences:

1. He felt the car **vibrate** and knew that the motor was going.
2. He could not **satiate** his appetite.
3. I do not question the **validity** of the document.
4. Our aim is to **nourish** the underfed children.
5. You **overwhelm** me with these attentions.
6. Mr. McKenzie will **verify** my remarks.
7. There were many **notable** persons present.
8. The name of the institution is of **secondary** importance.
9. Mrs. Noel's face assumed a **pensive** expression.
10. The mental **anguish** caused by this misfortune was inestimable.
11. I do not wish to **defile** the name of anyone.
12. We realized that we had set out on a **perilous** mission.
13. For general **utility,** you will find Mr. Cather valuable.
14. His loss of property was a serious **affliction.**
15. Mr. Lathrop did not **vacillate,** but remained steadfast in his opinion.
16. Remember, I do not **sanction** this act.

Exercise

1. Construct sentences containing the adverbial form of:

   overwhelm   **notable**   **secondary**

2. From what Latin words are these derived?

   satiate   **verify**   **sanction**

3. Write two synonyms for each of these words:

   anguish   **nourish**   **affliction**

4. Use in sentences:

   verification   **vibration**   **defilement**

67

Lesson 50

AVIATION TERMS

parachute	(păr'á shōōt)	A device for making a descent from a balloon or airplane.
hangar	(hăng'ẽr; hăng'gär)	A structure wherein airplanes are stored or housed.
dirigible	(dĭr'ĭ jĭ b'l)	An air vehicle, somewhat like a balloon, which can be directed.
glider	(glīd'ẽr)	An air machine without any motive power.
aeroplane	(ā'ẽr ŏ plān; âr'ŏ—)	A flying machine that is heavier than air and is self-propelled.
anemometer	(ăn ê mŏm'ê tẽr)	An instrument that measures the velocity of the wind.
fuselage	(fū'zĕ lȧj)	The place in an airplane where the pilot is seated, and where are found engine, controls, and other machinery.
aeronautics	(ā''ẽr ŏ nô'tĭks; âr''ŏ—)	The science of flying in the air, considered in its technical and theoretical aspects.
aviation	(ā vĭ ā'shŭn)	The practical art of flying.
altitude	(ăl'tĭ tūd)	Height; elevation above the ground.
hydroplane	(hī'drŏ plān)	A boat that glides on the surface of the water; a plane or fin of such a boat.
velocity	(vê lŏs'ĭ tĭ)	The speed of a machine.
biplane	(bī'plān)	An airplane with two wings, one above the other.
monoplane	(mŏn'ŏ—)	An airplane with one wing on a balancing surface.
ballast	(băl'ȧst)	Heavy material carried by a balloon or ship to steady it.

Exercise

1. How does a **monoplane** differ from a **biplane**? A **dirigible** from a **balloon**?

2. **Aeroplane** may have how many syllables?

68

Lesson 51

MISCELLANEOUS WORDS DEFINED AND ILLUSTRATED

fugitive	(fū′jĭ tĭv)	A runaway or deserter.
grumble	(grŭm′b'l)	To find fault; to murmur discontentedly.
foster	(fŏs′tẽr)	To nourish; to cherish; to support.
allegiance	(ă lē′jăns)	Devotion; the owing of loyalty.
calamity	(kă lăm′ĭ tĭ)	Disaster; extreme misfortune.
extensive	(ĕks tĕn′sĭv)	Comprehensive; far-reaching; wide.
affliction	(ăf flĭk′shŭn)	Great trouble; prolonged pain; ailment.
curiosity	(kū rĭ ŏs′ĭ tĭ)	Eager desire to know; inquisitiveness.
leisure	(lē′zhẽr; lĕzh′ẽr)	Spare time; an unemployed period.
appreciate	(ă prē′shĭ āt)	To value; to esteem properly; to increase in value.
inspiration	(ĭn spĭ rā′shŭn)	An act or influence stimulating the intellect or emotions.
antiquity	(ăn tĭk′wĭ tĭ)	Early ages; ancient times.

Words Illustrated

Each of the following sentences contains two words taken in order from the preceding list:

1. The chief of police **grumbled** a great deal when the **fugitive** from justice was not caught.
2. Teachers should **foster** in their pupils an **allegiance** to the flag.
3. **Extensive** plans have been made to aid all who suffered from the **calamity**.
4. The family's **affliction** caused much **curiosity**.
5. I shall **appreciate** a visit from you when you are at **leisure**.
6. It was an **inspiration** to listen to him relate incidents that dated back to the days of **antiquity**.

Exercise

Write sentences containing these words, which are related to words in the list above:

afflicted	extension	antiquated
calamitous	curious	appreciative

69

Lesson 52

AUTOMOBILE TERMS

chauffeur	(shŏ fûr´; shō´fĕr)	A man who drives an automobile.
chassis	(chăs´ĭ)	The under part of an automobile.
speedometer	(spĕd ŏm´ĕ tēr)	An instrument that indicates speed.
accelerator	(ăk sĕl´ĕr ā tēr)	A device for regulating the flow of gasoline and, thereby, the speed of a motorcar.
cyclometer	(sī klŏm´ĕ tēr)	An instrument that records the distance covered.
tonneau	(tŭn ō´)	The closed or upper part of an auto, in contrast with the chassis.
pneumatic	(nŭ măt´ĭk)	That which may be inflated with air, as a tire.
vulcanize	(vŭl´kăn īz)	To patch something (such as an auto tire) with crude rubber by applying heat.
transmission	(trăns mĭsh´ŭn)	Apparatus by which power is sent from engine to axle.
coupé	(kōō pā´)	A closed automobile for two, three, or four passengers.
inflate	(ĭn flāt´)	To swell with air or gas.
hydrometer	(hī drŏm´—)	A device for testing the strength of wet batteries.
garage	(gȧ räzh´)	A building where automobiles are kept.
reverse (v.)	(rĕ vẽrs´)	To turn back; to set going in the opposite direction.
detachable	(dĕ tăch´ȧ b'l)	Capable of being separated.
deflate	(dĕ flāt´)	To reduce the quantity of air or gas in some blown-up body.
insulate	(ĭn´sŭ lāt)	To cover with a material that will not conduct electricity, heat, or other form of energy.
carburetor	(kär´bŭ rĕt ēr)	Apparatus in which air and gasoline are mixed to form a mixture which may be exploded for power.
lubricant	(lū´brĭ kănt)	That which makes smooth or slippery.
traction	(trăk´shŭn)	Act of drawing a body along a surface.

TEST IV

(This test embraces material found in Lessons 39–52, inclusive.)

I. How are these words pronounced?

cordially	satiate	mischievous
athletic	longitude	combatant

II. Can you find three misspelled words in the following sentences?

1. He deemed it advisable to pay $1,000 on the principle.
2. Care should be taken to eat only digestable food.
3. The boy was not very accomodating to the visitors.
4. We could not ascertain what was the real grievance between them.

III. Write a word which is related to each of these words:

intricate	adversity	renovate
habitual	vagrant	humility
concede	antique	malicious

IV. Give two synonyms for:

separate	arrogant	emergency
firmness	slothful	liquidate

V. Select an adjective from Group 1 and apply it correctly to a noun from Group 2.

Group 1

1. unswerving
2. intricate
3. strenuous
4. exquisite
5. perilous
6. abject
7. impetuous
8. malicious

Group 2

1. poverty
2. statement
3. temper
4. undertaking
5. problem
6. allegiance
7. taste
8. opposition

71

Lesson 53

FAMILY, OR RELATED, WORDS

Words which have the same word-roots are called family, or related, words. A knowledge of the word-root will enable you to ascertain the meaning of the verb and of the related noun or adjective.

Verb	Meaning	Noun	Adjective
collect	To gather.	collection	collective
profess	To declare.	profession	professional
oppress	To burden.	oppression	oppressive
express	To utter.	expression	expressive
decide	To settle.	decision	decisive
produce	To bring forth.	production	productive
depress	To sadden.	depression	depressive
extend	To stretch out.	extension	extensive
define	To limit.	definition	definite
heal	To cure.	health	healthful
elect	To choose.	election	elective

Exercise

Find the basic word from which each of the boldfaced words is derived:

1. He could not give a **definite** reason why **production** had decreased.
2. The Elks are conducting an **extensive** charity campaign.
3. The life of a peasant was a continual round of **oppression**.
4. We should aim to make our speech more **expressive**.
5. The country has passed through a period of **depression**.
6. The climate of Florida is very **healthful**.
7. Dr. Brennan has failed to send me a bill for his **professional** services.
8. The Battle of Verdun was a **decisive** victory for the Allies.
9. Such **oppressive** measures were bound to prove unpopular.
10. Mr. Grafton's manner of teaching was **productive** of much good.
11. The office of mayor is an **elective** one.

Lesson 54

FAMILY, OR RELATED, WORDS

The words of Groups II and III are derived from the basic words in Group I.

Group I	Meaning	Group II	Group III
ardor	Zeal.	ardent	arduous
buoy	A float.	buoyancy	buoyant
alien	Foreign.	alienation	alienate
urban	Pertaining to a city.	urbanity	urbane
clear	Bright.	clarify	clarification
execute	To carry out.	executive	execution
image	Mental picture.	imagine	imaginary
gratify	To please.	grateful	gratitude
capture	To take.	captive	captivity
discern	To see clearly.	discernible	discernment
inhabit	To live in.	inhabitable	inhabitant
remit	To send back; to pardon.	remission	remittance

Exercise

Fill each blank with the appropriate form of the word which is found in parentheses:

1. The insincerity of the (**execute**) _____ (**alien**) _____ many of his friends.
2. I wish you would (**clear**) _____ that statement.
3. The (**inhabit**) _____ of this town are (**ardor**) _____ baseball enthusiasts.
4. The urban residents showed their (**grateful**) _____ to the mayor for what he had done for them.
5. The mistake was not (**discern**) _____ at first.
6. To capture the fortress proved an (**ardor**) _____ task.
7. He said, "We should be (**gratify**) _____ to the Almighty, for His unspeakable blessings."
8. St. Helena was Napoleon's place of (**capture**) _____.
9. His troubles were mostly (**image**) _____.

73

Lesson 55

WORDS AND THEIR DEFINITIONS

posterity	Future generations collectively.
achieve	To perform; accomplish; carry out.
anguish	Intense mental or physical suffering.
deliberate (*v.*)	To reflect on; think upon; consider.
astonishment	Extreme surprise; amazement.
perilous	Dangerous; hazardous.
obligation	Binding promise; duty.

Exercise

A. Fill the blanks with words taken from the list above:

1. The question is so important that I believe we should _____ upon it for a longer time.
2. To the _____ of the spectators, he performed the _____ act of going over Niagara Falls in a barrel.
3. The boy's failure caused his mother much _____.
4. We should try to _____ success, and hand it down to _____.
5. There is an _____ imposed upon every pupil to make good use of his time.

B. Give the verb from which **obligation** is derived, and also its adjective-form.

Multiple-Choice Exercise

Which of the three definitions given in each case is the appropriate one for the word?

tribunal	A court of justice; a theater; a contest.
ponder	To think about; to burden; to push.
fracas	An accident; an instrument; a quarrel.
hoard (*v.*)	To give away; to lay up money; to build.
trihedral	Having ten sides; having three sides; having two sides.
inflexible	Not to be bent; not to be solid; not to be broken.
beguile	To find fault with; to nourish; to deceive.
populate	To vote; to inhabit; to scold.
modify	To change; to dress; to paint.

74

Lesson 56

FAMILY, OR RELATED, WORDS

In an earlier exercise the simplest form of related-word groups was a verb. The basic words in this group are adjectives.

Adjective	Meaning	Verb	Noun
fertile	Fruitful.	fertilize	fertility
pure	Clean.	purify	purity
certain	Sure.	certify	certainty
real	Existing.	realize	reality
solid	Firm.	solidify	solidity
false	Untrue.	falsify	falsity
special	Particular.	specialize	specialty
social	Friendly.	socialize	society
legal	Lawful.	legalize	legality
equal	Uniform.	equalize	equality
vital	Full of life.	vitalize	vitality
immortal	Deathless.	immortalize	immortality

Exercise

Name the adjective-form of each of the boldfaced words:

1. Mr. Brophy **certified** my check.
2. There is a vast difference between truth and **falsity.**
3. It was due to his strong **vitality** that he survived the operation.
4. Some states have **legalized** Sunday baseball-playing.
5. We have no certainty that our wages will be **equalized.**
6. **Socialized** recitations form a part of our high-school course of studies.
7. Many taxpayers questioned the **legality** of the mayor's act.
8. Mr. Allen's wish for a new school will soon become a **reality.**
9. The tendency among doctors now is to **specialize** in certain diseases.
10. Religion teaches the **immortality** of the soul.
11. We have no **certainty** that the man will arrive tomorrow.
12. What body of people resolved to **purify** religion?
13. A good teacher tries to **vitalize** his recitations.

Lesson 57

FAMILY, OR RELATED, WORDS

In these groups the basic words are various parts of speech, such as an adjective, a noun, or a verb:

Group I	Meaning	Group II	Group III
sympathy	Compassion.	sympathize	sympathetic
pacific	Peaceful.	pacify	pacification
terror	Fright.	terrorize	terrible
explode	To burst forth.	explosion	explosive
constitute	To make, compose.	constitution	constituent
locate	To place.	localize	location
compel	To force.	compelling	compulsion
antique	Very old.	antiquity	antiquated
vary	To change.	variety	variable
author	The originator.	authorize	authority
signal	Sign.	signalize	signification
mobile	Movable.	mobilize	mobility

Exercise

Fill each blank with the appropriate form of the word which is given in parentheses:

1. The (constitute) _____ groups did not agree at the meeting.
2. Mary has a very (sympathy) _____ nature.
3. Strenuous efforts were made to (pacific) _____ the combatants.
4. Have you (author) _____ to discuss this subject with me?
5. Her taste is too (antique) _____.
6. Many persons are afflicted with colds due to our (vary) _____ climate.
7. His (explode) _____ wrath was the subject of conversation.
8. The (vary) _____ weather of New England causes much illness.
9. It was a (compel) _____ sense of duty that prompted him to cast his lot with the Tories.
10. The boy could not tell the exact (locate) _____ of the wreck.
11. The firing at Bunker Hill (signal) _____ the beginning of the Revolutionary War.
12. Mr. Greeley was (author) _____ to discuss peace terms with the labor union representatives.

MISCELLANEOUS WORDS WITH COMPLETION EXERCISE

defer	(dĕ fûr′)	To put off; delay; yield.
odious	(ō′dĭ ŭs)	Offensive; unpopular.
urgent	(ûr′jĕnt)	Pressing; calling for quick action.
adjust	(ă jŭst′)	To settle satisfactorily; make exact.
tendency	(tĕn′dĕn sĭ)	Inclination; disposition.
admonish	(ăd mŏn′ĭsh)	To warn; to caution; to reprove.
superfluous	(sū pûr′floō ŭs)	Unnecessary; more than needed.
rebellious	(rĕ bĕl′yŭs)	Opposing lawful authority.

Exercises

A. Fill each blank with an appropriate word taken from the preceding list:

1. There was an _____ need for prudent action during the riot.
2. The present trouble between the manufacturers and the laborers will be _____ this month.
3. The principal _____ the pupils against destroying school property.
4. A person who has a _____ to stay in bed too long will always be late.
5. The orator's remarks in regard to his own experiences were _____.
6. It was decided to _____ action on the motion until the next meeting.
7. The teacher found it impossible to cure the boy of his _____ spirit.
8. During the election, _____ propaganda was circulated by the different parties.

B. To which words in the list above are the boldfaced words related?

1. Out of **deference** to his superiors, he agreed to remain.
2. The unruly boy paid no attention to my words of **admonition.**
3. There was a great **urgency** for his being present at the meeting.
4. Was there an **adjustment** of accounts?
5. His speech was full of **superfluities.**

Lesson 59

WORD-ROOTS AND PREFIXES

Exercise

In the following sentences select the root and the prefix of the boldfaced words, and show how the latter affects the meaning:

1. Every attempt was made to **avert** the disaster.
2. Many people **abstain** from eating meat on Friday.
3. If one **adheres** to the principles of honesty and uprightness, he will succeed.
4. Kindly **affix** your signature to this petition.
5. The death of Webster **antedated** the Civil War.
6. Can you name the first man to **circumnavigate** the world?
7. There are 360 degrees in the **circumference** of a circle.
8. The members of the executive committee will **convene** in my office next Monday.
9. Mr. Hayward would like you to **correspond** with him.
10. One should be very cautious about **contradicting** what his superiors say.
11. An apology often **counteracts** the effects produced by malicious remarks.
12. The city intends to **divert** traffic from its central section.
13. I tried to **dissuade** him from delivering a speech against the system.
14. The unruly visitor was **ejected** from the meeting.
15. In these days, one can see many instances of **extravagance.**
16. His references to the misuse of public funds were considered **inappropriate** and unnecessary.
17. The smell of smoke **permeated** the atmosphere of the classroom.
18. **Posterity** will greatly profit by the wonderful inventions of this era.
19. Fair weather has been **predicted** for tomorrow.
20. An attempt has been made by the school to **revive** the athletic spirit of past years.
21. We should be willing at all times to **subordinate** our pleasures to those of our parents.
22. A foreman has been hired to **supervise** the work.

Lesson 60

MISCELLANEOUS WORDS

authentic	(ô thĕn′tĭk)	Original; true; trustworthy.
relegate	(rĕl′ē gāt)	To move back or to an inferior place.
allege	(ă lĕj′)	To affirm; to declare; to assert.
rarity	(răr′ĭ tĭ)	A choice or scarce article.
querulous	(kwĕr′ū lŭs)	Faultfinding; fretful.
decrepit	(dē krĕp′ĭt)	Feeble with age; worn out.
turmoil	(tûr′moil)	Agitation; tumult; noise.
garrulous	(găr′ū lŭs)	Talkative; wordy; loquacious.
assuage	(ă swāj′)	To soften or soothe; to lessen.
schism	(sĭzm)	A split or division.
adherent	(ăd hē′rĕnt)	One who holds fast to.
construe	(kŏn strōō′)	To translate; explain.
timorous	(tĭm′ēr ŭs)	Fearful of danger.
jocular	(jŏk′ū lår)	Making jokes; done in jest.
compunction	(kŏm pŭnk′shŭn)	Grief occasioned by guilt.
anonymous	(ă nŏn′ĭ mŭs)	Of unknown name or authorship.
detriment	(dĕt′rĭ mĕnt)	A hindrance; loss; drawback.
competent	(kŏm′pē tĕnt)	Capable; able; qualified.
precision	(prē sĭ′zhŭn)	Accuracy; correctness.
circulate	(sēr′kŭ lāt)	To pass from one person to another.
prudence	(prōō′dĕns)	Wisdom; foresight; caution.
discretion	(dĭs krĕ′shŭn)	Judgment; choice; use of prudence.
sanguine	(săng′gwĭn)	Inclined to be hopeful; sure.
fictitious	(fĭk tĭ′shŭs)	Assumed; false; not real.

Exercise

1. Construct sentences with:

assuage	timorous	precision
discretion	querulous	compunction

2. How is **schism** pronounced?

3. What are the adjectival forms of these words?

rarity	prudence	precision

WORDS SIMILAR IN SOUND WHICH ARE OFTEN CONFUSED

Word	Meaning	Example
scent	Odor.	The scent of roses filled the room.
sent	Dispatched.	The boy was sent on an errand.
decease (*n.*)	Death.	The decease of the President was mourned.
disease	Illness.	He died of a lingering disease.
except (*prep.*)	Omitting.	All except Anna attended the affair.
accept (*v.*)	Receive.	The judge would not accept the testimony.
populace	People.	The populace demanded daylight saving.
populous	Crowded.	New York is a populous city.
prophesy	To foretell.	I prophesy success for the ambitious student.
prophecy	What is foretold.	The old man's prophecy was not fulfilled.
attendance	Presence.	His attendance at school was irregular.
attendants	Those who serve another.	The queen's attendants were very loyal and courteous.
rite	Ceremony.	The funeral rites were well attended.
right	Correct.	He failed to get the right answer.
pair	Two.	He bought a pair of shoes.
pare	To remove the outer skin.	I helped mother pare the potatoes.

WORDS SIMILAR IN SOUND WHICH ARE OFTEN CONFUSED

Word	*Meaning*	*Example*
bowlder	Rock.	It required two horses to move the **bowlder**.
bolder	More audacious.	The child becomes **bolder** each day.
feint	Pretense.	His threat was only a **feint**.
faint	Weak.	Mary felt **faint** after her siege of sickness.
cession	Yielding (of rights).	By the **cession** of the Philippine Islands Spain lost a foothold in the East.
session	Meeting.	There was no court **session** today.
frieze	Ornamental band on a wall.	The **frieze** depicted a scene of the war.
freeze	To harden by cold.	Water will **freeze** at 32 degrees.
shear	To cut or snip.	The owner will **shear** the wool from his sheep.
sheer	Absolute, utter.	He failed in his test through **sheer** laziness.
hew	To chop.	The men have commenced to **hew** down the trees.
hue	Color.	Her hat was of a greenish **hue**.
cannon	Large gun.	The **cannon** roared.
canon	Law.	A **canon** of the church was violated.
gilt	Like gold.	There was a **gilt** frame around the picture.
guilt	Blame or crime.	His actions were an admission of **guilt**.
assent	Agree.	His father would not **assent** to the plan.
ascent	Rising.	The airplane's **ascent** was a failure.
need	Lack or want.	There is a **need** for deep thinkers.
knead	To press with the hands.	Mother is going to **knead** some bread dough.
creek	Body of water.	The boys are swimming in the **creek**.
creak	Squeaking sound.	We could hear the **creak** of wheels.

Lesson 63

WORDS SIMILAR IN SOUND WHICH ARE OFTEN CONFUSED

Word	*Meaning*	*Example*
access	Approach.	He did not have **access** to the office.
excess	Amount over.	Think of a number in **excess** of ten.
sleight	Trick.	Keller was a **sleight**-of-hand artist.
slight	Small.	He received only a **slight** reward for his bravery.
profit	Gain.	We should **profit** by experience.
prophet	Wise man who fore-tells.	A **prophet** is not always appreciated in his home town.
pedal	A foot lever.	The bicycle had a broken **pedal**.
peddle	To sell or distribute.	We should not **peddle** news of a slanderous type.
confidant	An intimate friend.	Colonel House was Wilson's **confidant**.
confident	Sure, positive.	The young athlete was **confident** of victory.
bullion	Uncoined gold or silver.	The **bullion** was taken to the mint for coinage.
bouillon	A clear broth.	The **bouillon** was too hot.
eminent	Distinguished.	The **eminent** Mr. Jones is dead.
imminent	Threatening.	A storm is **imminent**.
incite	Arouse.	Such talk will **incite** them to fight.
insight	Understanding.	He has a deep **insight** into philosophy.

Exercise

Select the appropriate word:

1. Judging from the remarks that were hurled, we knew that trouble was (**eminent, imminent**).
2. His (**confident, confidant**) attitude often made victory easy.
3. Everything was done to (**insight, incite**) the man to action.

WORDS SIMILAR IN SOUND WHICH ARE OFTEN CONFUSED

Word	*Meaning*	*Example*
heard	Distinguished by the ear.	A voice was **heard** in the wilderness.
herd	Band (of cattle).	Two of the **herd** were killed by lightning.
medal	Inscribed metal disk.	He received a **medal** for his bravery.
meddle	To interfere.	Do not **meddle** in the affairs of another.
core	Heart, center.	The apple was rotten to the **core.**
corps	Band (of troops).	The first **corps** went for a hike.
mantle	Cloak.	She placed her **mantle** on the chair.
mantel	Shelf above a fireplace.	The picture was placed on the **mantel.**
marshal	Leader.	Smith was appointed field **marshal.**
martial	Warlike.	The man assumed a **martial** attitude.
hoard	To store secretly.	One should not **hoard** his money.
horde	Tribe.	A **horde** of robbers descended upon the city.
dual	Double.	He played a **dual** role.
duel	Fight between two persons.	It is unlawful to take part in a **duel.**
bad	Wicked, not good.	His motives were **bad.**
bade (*past of* **bid**)	Told, ordered.	I **bade** him adieu.
mettle	Courage.	He showed his **mettle** during the contest.
metal	A malleable substance.	The bell was made of fine **metal.**

WORDS SIMILAR IN SOUND WHICH ARE OFTEN CONFUSED

Word	*Meaning*	*Example*
canvas	Cloth.	The tent was made of **canvas**.
canvass (*v.*)	To solicit.	We shall **canvass** the city for money for the afflicted.
canvass (*n.*)	A survey.	We made a **canvass** of the city for votes.
miner	Mine worker.	The **miner** came up the mine shaft.
minor	One under legal age of maturity.	The **minor** could not obtain work.
council	Assembly.	The **council** will meet next week to decide the question.
counsel	Advice.	He refused to take any **counsel** from his friends.
coarse	Not refined.	His **coarse** talk was censured by his superiors.
course	Path, way.	The **course** lay between two fires of the enemy.
extent	Measure, amount.	The **extent** of the damage is not known.
extant	In existence.	The author's works are no longer **extant**.
fate	Destiny.	Napoleon's **fate** is known by all.
fete	Festival.	The **fete** was a great financial success.
wring (*v.*)	To force out.	We could not **wring** a confession from him.
ring (*n.*)	Circular band.	A gold **ring** was found in the yard.
raze	To destroy.	The fire **razed** the building to the ground.
raise	To lift up.	I **raised** my bedroom window.
principal (*n.*)	Leader.	The **principal** of the school was well educated.
principle	Rule of conduct.	"Never be late" is a good **principle** to follow.

WORDS SIMILAR IN SOUND WHICH ARE OFTEN CONFUSED

Word	Meaning	Example
plane	A level surface.	The desk surface is a **plane**.
plain (*adj.*)	Evident.	It is **plain** that you did not study your lesson.
plain (*n.*)	Level earth.	The city lay on a **plain**.
mean	Contemptible.	The child is not **mean**, but mischievous.
mien	Bearing, expression.	He was a man of dignified **mien**.
staid	Sober.	Mrs. Fern was a **staid** old lady.
stayed	Stopped.	My friends **stayed** to see the experiment.
serge	A twilled fabric.	The material was navy blue **serge**.
surge	Rush.	There was a **surge** of applicants when the doors opened.
stationery	Writing paper.	I left my **stationery** upstairs.
stationary	Fixed.	The tables in the store are **stationary**.
reference	Allusion.	No **reference** was made to his mistake.
reverence	Deep respect.	I have great **reverence** for a man who leads an upright life.
personal	Private.	This is my **personal** affair.
personnel	Body or group of persons.	No change was made in the **personnel** of the office.
affect	To influence, to assume.	He was deeply **affected** by his sister's death.
effect (*v.*)	To accomplish.	We could not **effect** a meeting with the mayor.
ingenuous	Frank.	His noble, **ingenuous** nature was well known.
ingenious	Talented, clever.	The inventor of this device was an **ingenious** person.

Exercise

Construct sentences with the verbs **affect** and **effect**.

TEST V

(This test embraces material found in Lessons 53–66, inclusive.)

I. Write a sentence containing the adjectival form of:

defiance	inhabit	antagonize
express	destroy	sympathy
extent	signify	oppression

II. What is the meaning of each word?

ingenious	timorous	precision
assuage	relegate	legality
ponder	achieve	temporary

III. Give an antonym for:

perilous	abolish	posterity

IV. Which of these statements are true and which are false?

1. Tranquillity is the noun-form of tranquil.
2. Generous is an antonym of bounteous.
3. Schism is pronounced as if it were spelled sizm.
4. Reproof means to a rewrite.
5. Seduce, produce, reduce, induce, and conduce are derived from the Latin word ducere.

V. Write a sentence containing each of the following:

air of compunction	radiant smile
period of depression	temporary relief
spirit of defiance	variable climate

VI. Illustrate in sentences the meaning of:

affect	canvas	extent	stationery
effect (v.)	canvass	extant	stationary

VII. Select the proper definition or definitions of the following:

principal (1) leader, (2) sum of money, (3) rule.
mantle (1) shelf, (2) fireplace, (3) cloak.
mettle (1) iron, (2) courage, (3) malleable substance.

Lesson 67

EXERCISES

A. In the following sentences there are seven words that are either misspelled or incorrectly used. Can you find them?

1. The pupil was placed in an embarrassing position when he was brought before teacher and parent.
2. The Red Cross workers will canvas the city for new members next week.
3. A case paralell to our own happened only recently.
4. The drummer was unable to find one of his cymbals.
5. An autoist should be able to guage distances in order to eliminate accidents.
6. The governor recommended that the prosecution be postponed for a month.
7. Each pupil should try to be as accomodating as possible to his superiors.
8. One hundred coal minors were killed when part of the mine caved in.
9. At the last cession of the assembly many bills were passed.
10. There is a stationary pole in front of the new stationery store.
11. The judge was unable to illicit any information from the prisoner.
12. Two leading artists took part in the musicale.

B. In each case, which of these spellings is correct?

I	II
wierd	weird
calendar	calender
receivor	receiver
ecstacy	ecstasy
harrass	harass
nickle	nickel
attendant	attendent
forgettable	forgetable
developement	development
embarrass	embarass

MISCELLANEOUS TERMS (DOMESTIC SCIENCE, ART, HYGIENE, ETC.)

This list contains terms pertaining to domestic science, art, history, agriculture, physiology, and hygiene. Learn the spelling and meaning of each word, and then tell to which field it belongs.

circulation	economics	fertilizer
descendant	sterilize	sanitation
mercerized	horticulture	respiration
bacteria	nutrition	contraband
assessment	infection	pulverize
intestinal	consistency	fumigate
incubation	dairying	husbandry
embroidery	laboratory	appropriation
capillary	referendum	international
unanimous	cafeteria	minority
tillage	nitrogen	renovate
crochet	gelatin	pasteurize
plurality	corpuscle	proportions
diaphragm	linoleum	proclamation
utensil	nominate	ratification
resignation	porosity	jurisdiction
prosecution	adulteration	supremacy
nutrient	spraying	reconstruction
absorption	sediment	coagulated
albumen	treachery	pollination

Exercise

1. How did **pasteurize** receive its name?

2. Is every **infectious** disease contagious?

3. Explain the difference between **plurality** and **majority**.

88

TERMS USED IN ARITHMETIC, HISTORY, SCIENCE, AND GRAMMAR

Each of these words pertains to one of four fields: arithmetic, history, science, or grammar. Learn the spelling and meaning of each word, and state to which field it belongs.

equation	allegiance	multiplicand
syllable	transpose	arbitration
amnesty	respiration	circumference
quotient	conqueror	disintegrate
alliance	equilateral	indefinite
solution	pigment	numerical
evolution	diagonal	annexation
construct	affirmative	perpendicular
symbol	accuracy	counterfeit
domain	franchise	synonyms
pressure	diffusion	experiment
negative	vocabulary	entanglements
fugitive	percentage	combatant
vertical	dependency	ventilation
modify	synthesis	enterprise
stratum	phenomenon	subtrahend
document	lubricate	aristocracy
translucent	filibuster	phosphorus
conditional	neutralize	subordinate
salutation	mispronounce	condensation

Exercise

1. How is **combatant** pronounced?
2. Give the plural of **stratum**.
3. Explain the difference between a **synonym** and an antonym.
4. Is a square an **equilateral** figure?

Lesson 70

RADIO TERMS

antenna		An elevated wire, or wires, stretched in the air for transmitting or receiving high-frequency electric waves.
microphone		An instrument for transmitting sounds.
amplifier		A device which renders sounds louder or more intense, or makes them carry farther.
condenser		An appliance which concentrates electricity.
reception		Admission; acceptance.
frequency	(frē′kwĕn sĭ)	Occurrence often repeated; vibrations per second.
audibility	(ô dĭ bĭl′ĭ tĭ)	Capability of being heard.
tuning		Giving tone to; sounding.
aerial	(â ē′rĭ al; âr′—)	Of or pertaining to the air.
resistance		Opposition of a substance to the passage through it of an electric current.
transmitter		That portion of an instrument by which a message is sent.
static		That which interferes with the satisfactory production of sound.
transformer		An apparatus for converting high-powered electric current to low, or vice versa.
interference		Intermixing of electric waves, causing confusion.
audition		Act of hearing.
broadcasting		Transmission of news, music, and the like, to many listeners by radio.

Exercise

Explain the bold-type words, which have been taken from an advertisement:

My radio is an **eight-tube** set, with a **dynamic** speaker. It is equipped with **phonograph attachment** and an **illuminated single dial** with a single **tuning** knob. It is set in a beautiful walnut **console**.

Lesson 71

RULES FOR SYLLABICATION

The subject of dividing words into syllables is so important as to warrant its being used as a separate lesson.

Here are some of the more important rules:

1. When two or more consecutive vowels represent a diphthong, as, for example, **oi, ai, ea, au,** etc., they are not separated, but are treated as a single vowel. Thus, one should never divide **oil, gait, eat, mount,** and other similar words.

2. Two consecutive vowels that are sounded separately, however, belong to separate syllables, as, for example, in **a or ta, a e ri al, sci ence, cur i ous.**

3. Certain consonants should not end syllables. This is usually true of **c** and **g** when soft, as in **wa ger, ex i gen cy, in vin ci ble.** C and g will, however, end a syllable when coming before an English suffix, as in **rang er, del ug ing,** etc.

4. Certain consonants should not begin a syllable. This is true of **x** when pronounced like **ks** or **gs,** as in **anx ious, exam ine, com plex ion;** and of **r** when preceded by **a** or **e,** or their equivalents, as in **par ent, fair est, av er age, gen er al.**

5. Generally recognized prefixes and suffixes are separated from the body of the word, as **-er, -est, -ing, -ist, -ish** in such words as **sweet er, smart est, chid ing, sweet ish.** When the last letter of the word is doubled before a suffix, however, the added letter goes with the suffix, as in **swim ming.**

6. When a single consonant comes between two sounded vowels, it usually joins the following vowel, as in **ko dak, fa vor, in va lid, no ti fy.**

7. When two consonants come between two sounded vowels, if the first vowel is long and accented, they join the following vowel, as in **en a bling, sa cred, peo ple, fee ble.** If the first vowel is short, one consonant may join it, as in **tab let, es teem, ves tige.**

Inasmuch as business heads assert that many of their clerks insist on dividing diphthongs, note the following:

laugh ing	feud al	seiz ing
guin ea	read a ble	tur moil

Lesson 72

SYLLABICATION

Exercise

Divide these words into syllables and mark the accent, thus:

la'dy	lem on ade'	re mark'ing	ben'e fit
perform	aversion	western	chocolate
question	personage	chiefly	entertain
dinner	anxiety	estate	monument
raisin	initiate	random	tiresome
attention	necessitate	November	persevere
imagine	charitable	performer	underpay
humane	interrupt	hospital	arithmetic
catalogue	divisible	intention	diameter
greediness	apprehension	character	recommend
primitive	grammatical	intercede	preparation
primarily	exploitation	associate	changeable

Words Illustrated

Some words from the list above are here used in sentences:

1. Too much work for the past year **necessitated** his taking a long rest.
2. I shall **intercede** for the young boy who is in trouble.
3. If you **persevere** in your work, you will surely succeed.
4. There was great **anxiety** in this country during Lindbergh's flight across the ocean.
5. Gregory's power of **apprehension** was responsible for his being first in his class.
6. Nearly every mother's mind is filled with **apprehension** when her son is playing football.

Exercise

Write sentences containing the verb-form of:

preparation   exploitation   apprehension

Lesson 73

WORDS OFTEN MISPRONOUNCED

In order to attain correct pronunciation, consult the dictionary whenever you are in doubt about a word and its pronunciation, and then read it aloud in an original sentence. It would be well to form original sentences with the words found in the following list.

lamentable	Pitiable.	(lăm′ĕn tȧ b'l,	*not* lȧ mĕnt′ȧ b'l)
poinsettia	A flower.	(poin sĕt′ĭ ȧ,	*not* poin sĕt′ȧ)
alias	False name.	(ā′lĭ ăs,	*not* ȧ lī′ăs)
faucet	Spigot.	(fô′sĕt,	*not* făs′ĕt)
centenary	One hundred years.	(sĕn′tĕ nĕr ĭ	*or* sĕn tĕn′ȧ rĭ)
respite	A brief rest.	(rĕs′pĭt,	*not* rē spīt′)
cognomen	Surname.	(kŏg nō′mĕn,	*not* kŏg′nŏ mĕn)
decade	Ten years.	(dĕk′ād,	*not* dē kād′)
abdomen	Part of the body.	(ăb dō′mĕn	*or* ăb′dŏ mĕn)
coadjutor	Helper.	(kŏ ăj′o͝o tẽr	*or* kō ȧ jo͞o′tẽr)
infamous	Of bad reputation.	(ĭn′fȧ mŭs,	*not* ĭn fā′mŭs)
quintuplet	One of five.	(kwĭn′tû plĕt,	*not* kwĭn tū′plĕt)
finance	Science of money.	(fĭ năns′	*or* fī′năns)
ordeal	Trial, test.	(ôr dē′ăl	*or* ôr′dē ăl)

Cautions

Note:

That **poinsettia** has four syllables.
That **decade** is accented on the first syllable.
That **respite** is accented on the first syllable.
That **centenary, abdomen, coadjutor, finance** (noun), and **ordeal** may now be pronounced in two different ways.

Exercise

Read aloud:

1. There was a **respite** of an hour during the fight.
2. We have been studying safety for more than a **decade.**
3. Mr. Jones, **alias** William Brown, was arrested.

Lesson 74

WORDS OFTEN MISPRONOUNCED

reptile	(rĕp′tĭl)	A crawling animal.
memorable	(mĕm′ȯ rȧ b'l)	Not to be forgotten.
dishevel	(dĭ sḥĕv′ĕl)	To disarrange.
status	(stā′tŭs)	Relative position; rank.
trough	(trȯf)	A shallow receptacle for water or other substance.
acclimated	(ȧ klī′mĭ tĕd; ăk′lĭ mā tĕd)	Accustomed to temperature or other condition.
despicable	(dĕs′pĭ kȧ b'l)	Mean; contemptible.
combatant	(kŏm′bȧ tănt)	One who fights in a battle or for a cause.
financier	(fĭn ăn sēr′; fī—)	One skilled in banking.
hospitable	(hŏs′pĭ tȧ b'l)	Generous in entertaining friends or strangers.
implacable	(ĭm plā′kȧ b'l; ĭm plăk′—)	Not to be appeased; unrelenting.
quay	(kē)	A firmly built wharf.
jugular	(jŭg′ṷ lẽr; jōō′gṷ—)	Pertaining to the neck.
desultory	(dĕs′ŭl tȯ rĭ)	Aimless, disconnected.
conversant	(kŏn′vẽr sănt)	Acquainted or familiar with.
zoology	(zō ŏl′ȯ jĭ)	Science of animal life.

Exercises

A. From what words are these derived?

memorable	acclimated	combatant
implacable	despicable	financier

B. Name four words in the above list which permit of two pronunciations.

C. Read aloud:

1. The superintendent criticized him for his **desultory** work.
2. He was quite **conversant** with the rules of the game.
3. The **combatants** agreed to meet at the **quay.**
4. A New Englander finds it difficult to become **acclimated** to the heat of Florida.
5. Aaron Burr was Hamilton's **implacable** foe.
6. We met many **hospitable** people during our trip.

Lesson 75

WORDS OFTEN MISPRONOUNCED

Many of the words in this list, which have been taken from the French language, still retain the foreign pronunciation:

buffet	(boॅo fā′)	A sideboard; refreshment counter.
masseur	(mă sûr′)	A man who massages the body.
chauffeur	(shŏ fûr′)	An operator of an automobile.
bouquet	(boॅo kā′)	A bunch of flowers.
prestige	(prĕs tēzh′)	Authority; influence or power.
boudoir	(boॅo′dwär)	A small dressing room.
trousseau	(troॅo′sō)	A bride's outfit.
mirage	(mĭ räzh′)	Something seen falsely; an optical illusion.
bouillon	(boॅo yôn′)	A kind of clear soup.
résumé	(rā zü mā′)	A summary.
fiancé	(fē än sā′)	A man to whom a woman is betrothed.
blasé	(blȧ zā′)	Wearied by too much pleasure; difficult to interest.
entree	(än trā′)	Entrance; a dish served between courses.
reservoir	(rĕz′ẽr vwôr)	A pool or basin where water or other reserve is stored.
de luxe	(dĕ lüks′)	Made unusually fine; luxurious.
sabotage	(sȧ bŏ tȧzh′)	Willful destruction of machinery or materials by workmen.

Cautions

1. Do not confuse **bouillon,** a clear soup, with **bullion,** uncoined precious metal.

2. **Buffet** may also be pronounced **bŭf′et,** though this is not so common as **boॅo fā′.**

Exercises

1. What is the feminine form of **fiancé?** **Masseur?**

2. Is **bouquet** ever pronounced **bō′kā** or **bō kā′?**

3. How was the word **sabotage** frequently used during the World War?

4. Are **résumé** and **epitome** synonymous terms?

5. Give three automobile terms derived from the French, in addition to **chauffeur.**

95

Lesson 76

WORDS HAVING TWO PRONUNCIATIONS

There are many words in the English language that permit of two or more pronunciations. Webster's New International Dictionary, Second Edition, is the source used here.

Word	Meaning	Pronunciation
survey (*n.*)	Examination.	(sûr′vā *or* sûr vā′)
illustrate	To picture.	(ĭl′ŭs trāt *or* ĭ lŭs′trāt)
gaping	Yawning.	(gāp′ĭng *or* gäp′ĭng)
envelope (*n.*)	Wrapper.	(ĕn′vĕ lŏp *or* ŏn′vĕ lŏp)
pianist	Player of the piano.	(pĭ ăn′ĭst *or* pē′á nĭst)
irrefutable	Not to be disputed.	(ĭr rĕf′ů tá b′l *or* ĭr rĕ fūt′á b′l)
peremptory	Decisive; imperative.	(pĕr ĕmp′tŏ rĭ *or* pĕr′ĕmp to′rĭ)
advertisement	A public notice.	(ăd vûr′tĭz mĕnt *or* ăd vûr tīz′mĕnt)
squalor	Dirty or untidy state.	(skwŏl′ẽr *or* skwā′lẽr)
demonstrate	To point out; to show.	(dĕm′ŭn strāt *or* dĕ mŏn′strāt)
isolate	To place by itself.	(ī′sŏ lāt *or* ĭs′ŏ lāt)
domicile	Residence.	(dŏm′ĭ sĭl *or* dŏm′ĭ sīl)

Exercise

Read aloud these sentences, which contain words from the preceding list, and endeavor to use the preferred pronunciation in each case.

1. I shall try to **illustrate** what I mean.
2. Kindly write the address on this **envelope.**
3. The convention found Patrick Henry's arguments **irrefutable.**
4. I read the **advertisement** to which you referred.
5. The principal's **peremptory** answer put an end to further questions.
6. Mr. Skehan **demonstrated** how to use the adding machine.

WORDS OF THE 4,000–5,000 POSITION IN THORNDIKE'S LIST

abound	chastise	cemetery	reflection
cereal	announce	mournful	additional
morsel	martyr	admissive	misfortune
afflict	ransom	plentiful	profitable
charter	pressure	challenge	signature
rascal	prophesy	adoption	performance
anguish	splendor	reception	intelligent
cherish	prudent	community	advertise
refrain	obstacle	objection	certificate
preside	needless	apartment	complexion
piety	obedient	confident	murderer
cleanse	painful	masculine	simplicity
refresh	primary	spiritual	management
circuit	solace	rectangle	illustrate
prairie	notable	nonsense	congratulate
confide	physical	stillness	imagination
quaint	partial	petition	exploration
resist	nourish	reference	dedicate
spurn	internal	literary	conspiracy
compact	leisure	confidence	attraction
sleigh	malice	magnify	banishment
siege	interpret	implement	artificial
clatter	exploit	expression	lamentation
vulgar	interval	financial	mountainous

Exercise

1. Use these words in sentences:

   interval   partial   conspiracy   magnify

2. Construct sentences with:

lament	lamentable	lamentation
dedicate	dedicatory	dedication
confident	confidential	confidence

WORDS OFTEN MISPRONOUNCED

pretense	False act or appearance.	(prĕ tĕns′	*or* prē′tĕns)
casualty	Accident, fatality.	(kăzh′ū ăl tĭ,	*not* căs ū ă′lĭ tĭ)
pumpkin	A gourdlike fruit.	(pŭmp′kĭn,	*not* pŭnk′ĭn)
amenable	Responsible; tractable.	(ȧ mē′nȧ b'l	*or* ȧ mĕn′ ȧ b'l)
reparable	Capable of being adjusted or compensated.	(rĕp′ȧ rȧ b'l,	*not* rĕ pâr′ȧ b'l)
vagrant	A wanderer, tramp.	(vā′grănt,	*not* văg′rănt)
cranberry	A red, edible berry.	(krăn′bĕr ĭ,	*not* krăm′ bĕr ĭ)
bade (*past tense of* **bid**)	Ordered; told.	(băd,	*not* bād)
combative	Pugnacious.	(kŏm′bȧ tĭv	*or* kŏm băt′ĭv)
appreciative	Showing understanding or true estimation.	(ȧ prē′shĭ ā′tĭv	*or* ȧ prē′shĭ ȧ tĭv)
discourse (*v.*)	To talk or converse.	(dĭs kōrs′,	*not* dĭs′kōrs)
hearth	Fireside.	(härth,	*not* hûrth)
viands	Edibles; food.	(vī′ănds,	*not* vē′ănds)
comely	Graceful; good-looking.	(kŭm′lĭ,	*not* kōm′lĭ)
amicable	Friendly.	(ăm′ĭ kȧ b'l,	*not* ȧ mĭk′ȧ b'l)
gist	Main point.	(jĭst,	*not* ghĭst)

Exercise

Write sentences containing these words:

discourse (*v.*)	pretense
amicable	gist
vagrant	bade
appreciative	combative

Lesson 79

EXERCISES IN PRONUNCIATION

Read aloud the following sentences, each of which contains a word frequently mispronounced:

1. There was no **pretense** in her manner.
2. The **casualty** was reported at 9 A.M.
3. The **pumpkin** is much in evidence at Thanksgiving.
4. He considered himself **amenable** to no one.
5. His loss was the more bitter because it was not **reparable.**
6. I was grieved to learn that he had become a mere **vagrant.**
7. The **cranberry** season was at its height.
8. Mrs. Suther **bade** me good-night at an early hour.
9. Seeing that he was in a **combative** mood, I soon left.
10. She was very **appreciative** of all that had been done.
11. It was always a pleasure to hear her **discourse,** for she had a knowledge of many subjects.
12. It was a cold night, and we were gathered around the **hearth.**
13. There was always an assortment of **viands** from which to choose.
14. She was a woman of **comely** appearance.
15. Let us try to reach an **amicable** settlement of the question.
16. At any rate, I have given you the **gist** of his talk.

Cautions

Care should be taken in pronunciation:

1. To sound the second **p** in **pumpkin;**
2. To use **n,** and not **m,** in **cranberry;**
3. Always to accent **discourse** (*v.*) on the last syllable.

Questions

1. Are **reparable** and **comparable** derived from the same root?
2. How is **g** pronounced before **i?** Before **a?**
3. In what way does a **discourse** differ from an ordinary **talk** or a **speech?**
4. Give a synonym for:

casualty   **hearth**   **pretense**   **vagrant**

Lesson 80

WORDS HAVING TWO PRONUNCIATIONS

Word	Meaning	Pronunciation
mobilize	To gather.	(mō'bǐ līz *or* mŏb'ǐ līz)
dictate	To tell or order.	(dǐk'tāt *or* dǐk tāt')
enervate	To weaken.	(ĕn'ẽr vāt *or* ĕ nûr'vāt)
nicotine	A poison in tobacco.	(nǐk'ô tēn *or* nǐk'ô tǐn)
patronage	Special support.	(pā'trŭn ǐj *or* pǎt'rŭn ǐj)
exemplary	Commendable.	(ĕg zĕm'plá rǐ *or* ĕg'zĕm plĕr ǐ)
rarity	Infrequency.	(rǎr'ǐ tǐ *or* râr'ǐ tǐ)
virile	Manlike.	(vǐr'ǐl *or* vī'rǐl)
economical	Thrifty.	(ē'kô nŏm ǐ kǎl *or* ĕk'ô nŏm ǐ kǎl)
detour	Roundabout way.	(dĕ tōŏr' *or* dē'tōŏr)
equable	Proportionate.	(ĕk'wá b'l *or* ē'kwá b'l)
languor	Weariness.	(lăng'gẽr *or* lăng'gwẽr)
apparent	Easily seen.	(ă pǎr'ĕnt *or* ă pâr'ĕnt)
misconstrue	To misinterpret.	(mǐs kǒn strōō' *or* mǐs kǒn'strōō)
juvenile	Youthful.	(jōō'vê nǐl *or* jōō'vĕn īl)
defalcation	Dishonest use of funds.	(dē'fǎl kā'shŭn *or* dĕf'ǎl kā'shŭn)

Exercise

A. Read aloud:

1. It was **apparent** that the governor would order the troops to be **mobilized.**
2. Autoists endeavor to avoid **detours.**
3. To live in the country is more **economical** than to live in the city.
4. It was a **rarity** to see Mr. Skehan angry.
5. Mr. Russell received great praise from the school board for his **exemplary** work.
6. I believe you have **misconstrued** my remark.
7. Loss of sleep is very **enervating** to both young and old.

Lesson 81

WORDS OFTEN MISPRONOUNCED

Exercise

A. In the following sentences there are words which are frequently mispronounced, even by college graduates. Having read aloud each sentence, turn to the next lesson to ascertain the number of these words you have pronounced correctly.

1. With each pound of coffee, a gift-coupon will be presented.
2. He made a grievous mistake in communicating his plans to his friends.
3. The teacher asked me to give an epitome of yesterday's story.
4. Many inquiries relative to the patient's condition came in.
5. France and Italy were allies during the World War.
6. Mary wore a yellow chrysanthemum on her coat.
7. The secretary gave an interesting account of his European trip.
8. Beginning next month, my new address will be 101 Washington Street.
9. The clerk was asked to procure as much data relative to the accident as possible.
10. Each adult attending the vaudeville performance received a circular.
11. The athlete soon realized that he was facing a formidable opponent.
12. The president addressed the club on the inadvisability of establishing such a precedent.

B. Here is a list of simple words which are frequently mispronounced. Check your pronunciation with that of the dictionary.

arctic	courteous	hostile	dictionary
comment (v.)	gratis	awkward	governor
influence	bureau	comely	boisterous
history	museum	probably	potatoes
recipe	tortoise	similar	umbrella
menu	regular	naturally	pumpkin
vase	chimney	genius	nuisance
apricot	familiar	forbade	raspberry

WORDS OFTEN MISPRONOUNCED

These words are found in the preceding section. Check your results for correct pronunciation.

coupon	A ticket.	(kōō′pŏn,	*never* kū′pŏn)
grievous	Serious, saddening.	(grē′vŭs,	*never* grē′vĭ ŭs)
epitome	A summary.	(ĕ pĭt′ŏ mē,	*never* ĕp′ĭ tōm)
inquiry	Investigation.	(ĭn kwīr′ĭ	*or* ĭn′kwĭ rĭ)
allies	Associates; confederates.	(ă līz′	*or* ăl′īz)
secretary	One who takes notes.	(sĕk′rĕ tĕr′ĭ	*or* sĕk′rĕ tă rĭ)
address (*n.*)	Place of residence; speech.	(ă drĕs′	*or* ăd′rĕs)
data	Facts (*plural*).	(dā′tȧ	*or* dä′tȧ)
adult	A grown-up person.	(ȧ dŭlt′	*or* ăd′ŭlt)
vaudeville	A miscellaneous show.	(vōd′vĭl	*or* vô′dĕ vĭl)
athlete	Person of strength.	(ăth′lēt,	*never* ăth′thē lēt)
address (*v.*)	To speak to.	(ă drĕs′,	*never* ă′drĕs)
precedent (*n.*)	Previous example.	(prĕs′ĕ dĕnt,	*never* prĕ sē′dĕnt)

Exercise

Read aloud these words, which are often mispronounced; then form sentences containing them:

address	inquiry	interesting
adult	grievous	vaudeville
allies	formidable	secretary

TEST VI

(This test embraces material found in Lessons 67–82, inclusive.)

I. Select the proper word.

1. I must purchase some (**stationary, stationery**).
2. Would you say Edison was an (**ingenious, ingenuous**) person?
3. We endeavored to (**effect, affect**) a meeting of the two candidates.
4. He acts on the (**principle, principal**) that honesty is the best policy.

II. Use in sentences:

sediment	diffusion	enterprise
fugitive	accuracy	perennial
audition	imperative	auxiliary

III. Pronounce:

alias	sinecure	implacable
respite	amicable	hospitable
allies	formidable	vaudeville

IV. Are any of the following pronunciations incorrect?

envelope	(ĕn'vĕ lōp)	(ŏn'vĕ lōp)
demonstrate	(dĕ mŏn'strāt)	(dĕm'ŭn strāt)
exemplary	(ĕg'zĕm plĕr ĭ)	(ĕg zĕm'plā rĭ)
enervate	(ĕ nûr'vāt)	(ĕn'ēr vāt)
irrefutable	(ĭr rĕf' û tá b'l)	(ĭr rĕ fūt'á b'l)

V. Syllabify:

secretary   despicable   memorable

VI. Write sentences containing:

desultory reading   formidable combatants
exemplary conduct   virile achievement
irreparable loss   amicable agreement

WORDS OFTEN MISPRONOUNCED

The most effective way to become acquainted with pronunciations is to hear oneself pronounce words aloud. Having studied the words on this page, read aloud the sentences in the next lesson.

harass	(hăr′ás)	To annoy; to worry.
orgy	(ôr′jĭ)	Revelry; immoderate indulgence.
long-lived	(lông-līvd)	Lasting; living to a great age.
requited	(rĕ kwī′tĕd)	Repaid; rewarded; returned.
longevity	(lŏn jĕv′ĭ tĭ)	Prolonged or lengthy life.
derisive	(dĕ rī′sĭv)	Expressing ridicule or scorn.
flaccid	(flăk′sĭd)	Flabby; soft.
chastisement	(chăs′tĭz mĕnt)	Punishment.
impious	(ĭm′pĭ ŭs)	Irreligious; wicked; irreverent.
strategic	(stră tē′jĭk)	Advantageous; done by artifice.
impotent	(ĭm′pŏ tĕnt)	Weak; without vigor.
incomparable	(ĭn kŏm′pá rá b'l)	Unequalled; beyond comparison.
obese	(ŏ bēs′)	Very fat; fleshy.
research	(rĕ sẽrch′)	Careful investigation.
genuine	(jĕn′ū ĭn)	Real; true; honest.

Cautions

Impious is never pronounced im pī′ŭs; nor genuine, jĕn′ū īn.
Note the spelling of harass and requited.
Harass may also be pronounced: há răs′.
Research may also be pronounced: rē′sûrch.

Exercise

1. Give the noun-form of derisive.
2. Write an antonym for impotent; for incomparable.
3. Why is the g soft in longevity?
4. Use in sentences:

unrequited love	harassed expression
incomparable good	impotent attack

Lesson 84

WORDS OFTEN MISPRONOUNCED

Exercises

A. Read aloud the following sentences, being sure to pronounce the bold-type words as they are accented in the preceding section.

1. Did the lawyer **harass** you with questions?
2. As soon as he received the money, he indulged in an **orgy** of spending.
3. All the members of my family are **long-lived.**
4. This deep feeling of friendship was not **requited.**
5. His **longevity** was due to the regularity of his living.
6. She was the object of many **derisive** remarks.
7. The child gazed with grief at the **flaccid** balloon.
8. We all felt that the **chastisement** was unjust.
9. His conduct in church was never **impious.**
10. It was a **strategic** move to attack at that time.
11. The occupant of the throne was an **impotent** ruler.
12. His poetry was considered **incomparable.**
13. She was **obese** but not clumsy.
14. His knowledge was the result of years of **research.**
15. The diamond was pronounced **genuine.**

B. Write sentences containing:

> **requital**   **strategy**   **derision**

C. What is the noun-form for each?

> **obese**   **impotent**   **strategic**

D. Construct sentences containing the following words:

> **research**   **incomparably**   **harass**
> **requited**   **strategic**   **orgy**
> **flaccid**   **derisive**   **impotent**

E. Use in sentences:

> **impious act**   **genuine grief**
> **available data**   **grievous offense**
> **exemplary work**   **potent influence**

105

Lesson 85

WORDS OFTEN MISPRONOUNCED

Amazing is the number of words that are mispronounced by educated people every day. The only effective remedy for this weakness, as we have noted before, is to resort constantly to the dictionary.

mischievous	(mĭs'chĭ vŭs,	*never* mĭs chē'vŭs)
interesting	(ĭn'tēr ĕs tĭng,	*never* ĭn tēr ĕst'ĭng)
epitome	(ė pĭt'ȯ mė,	*never* ĕp'ĭ tōm)
respite	(rĕs'pĭt,	*never* rė spīt')
arctic	(ärk'tĭk,	*never* är'tĭk)
faucet	(fô'sĕt,	*never* făs'ĕt)
discourse (*v.*)	(dĭs kōrs',	*never* dĭs'kōrs)
cognomen	(kŏg nō'mĕn,	*never* kŏg'nȯ mĕn)
combat (*n.*)	(kŏm'băt,	*never* kŏm băt')

Exercise

A. Find two mispronunciations in the following group.

applicable	Suitable.	(ăp'plĭ kȧ b'l)
hospitable	Friendly.	(hŏs'pĭ tȧ b'l)
implacable	Not to be appeased.	(ĭm plā'kȧ b'l)
infamous	Shameful, notorious.	(ĭn fā'mŭs)
heinous	Hateful, atrocious.	(hā'nŭs)
impotent	Powerless.	(ĭm'pȯ tĕnt)
conversant	Familiar.	(kŏn'vēr sănt)
gist	Pith of a matter.	(ghĭst)

B. Read aloud these sentences, focusing your attention on the bold-type words:

1. His grandparents are always **hospitable.**
2. The newspaper gave the **gist** of his speech.
3. This rule is **applicable** to percentage.
4. He was accused of a **heinous** crime.
5. Are you **conversant** with the uses of electricity?
6. I shall **discourse** upon "Good Books."
7. You should take a **respite** from your arduous work.

106

Lesson 86

WORDS OF MORE THAN ONE PRONUNCIATION

Let your aim be, in regard to words which have more than one pronunciation, to use the preferred form. Webster's International Dictionary, Second Edition, is the source of information recommended.

Word	Meaning	Pronunciation	
concentrate	To gather in a body.	(kŏn'sĕn trāt	*or* kŏn sĕn'trāt)
drama	Art of the stage; a play.	(drä'ma	*or* drăm'ả)
patron	A supporter.	(pā'trŭn	*or* păt'rŭn)
inundate	To overflow.	(ĭn'ŭn dāt	*or* ĭn ŭn'dāt)
prelude	Introduction.	(prĕl'ūd	*or* prē'lūd)
depot	Station for passengers or freight.	(dē'pō	*or* dā'pō)
inveigle	To entice.	(ĭn vē'g'l	*or* ĭn vā'g'l)
strategic	Pertaining to generalship; advantageous.	(strǎ tē'jĭk	*or* strǎ tĕj'ĭk)
reveille	Bugle-call at sunrise.	(rĕ vāl'yǎ	*or* rĕv ĕ lē')
hygiene	Science of health.	(hī'jēn	*or* hī'jĭ ēn)
leisure	Spare time.	(lē'zhûr	*or* lĕzh'ûr)
disputable	Able to be contested.	(dĭs'pū tả b'l	*or* dĭs pūt'ả b'l)
contemplate	To meditate on.	(kŏn'tĕm plāt	*or* kŏn tĕm'plāt)
surveillance	Close watch.	(sûr vāl'ăns	*or* sûr văl'yăns)
cynosure	Center of attraction.	(sī'nŏ shoor	*or* sĭn'ŏ shoor)

Exercise

Read aloud:

1. Do you **contemplate** a trip to Europe next year?
2. He could not be **inveigled** into voting for my candidate.
3. General Foch's **strategic** work is studied today in many military schools.
4. The **disputable** territory lay between the Nueces River and the Rio Grande.

Lesson 87

SOME CHANGES IN PRONUNCIATION

'The advent of the second edition of Webster's New International Dictionary affected the pronunciation of many words. Numerous pronunciations which were absolutely incorrect prior to September, 1934, are now correct.

Here are a few words which formerly had but one form, but now have two correct forms of pronunciation.

Read aloud the illustrations given for each word.

address   A formal discourse; the superscription of a letter.

No longer are the students restricted to placing the accent on the last syllable. It is now correct to say **address'** or **ad'dress.**

Who will deliver the main **address**?

My **address** is now 60 Chestnut Avenue.

inquiry   An investigation; a question.

It will be a source of pleasure to many to know that this word may now be accented on the first or the second syllable. Note how the second **i** is affected by the accent—**ĭn kwīr'ĭ,** or **ĭn'kwĭr ĭ.**

He could not answer my **inquiry.**

Such an **inquiry** must receive my attention.

alien   Foreign; strange.

It was considered a grave mistake to pronounce this word as one of three syllables. No more can that mistake occur, as the word now may have two or three syllables.

Many **aliens** are emigrating from our country.

Dishonesty was **alien** to his make-up.

sinecure   An office of value which requires little or no responsibility.

One is no longer obliged to have the first syllable rhyme with **dine;** it may also rhyme with **pin.**

The President's work is no **sinecure.**

The politicians distributed the **sinecures** among their friends.

secretary   A confidential clerk.

No more are we constrained to imitate the British sound of this word. It may now be **sec're tar'y;** that is, a secondary accent after the third syllable is now permissible.

A new **secretary** has been appointed.
The different **secretaries** met here yesterday.

jugular   Pertaining to the neck.

One may now pronounce the first syllable to rhyme with **mug** or to rhyme with **flue.**

Where is the **jugular** vein?
The **jugular** vein was cut.

ordeal   Trial; test.

It is now correct to place the accent on the first or second syllable of this word.

The early settlers underwent many **ordeals.**
I hope you will not consider this class an **ordeal.**

combat (*v.*)   To fight or contend against.

To say **combat'** for the verb is now permissible. One may accent the first or the second syllable of the verb-form and be correct. The noun-form of the word must be accented on the first syllable.

Let us **combat** the use of slang.
How shall we **combat** the depression?

ally (*n.*)   An associate; an auxiliary.

Although this word was invariably pronounced **al'ly,** this pronunciation was incorrect prior to September, 1934. Now, however, one may say either **ally'** or **al'ly** for the noun.

Who was his **ally** in this act?
Those boys are our stanchest **allies.**

data   Necessary information.

Formerly, it was necessary for the first syllable to rhyme with **bay;** now it is also correct to sound the first **a** like the **a** in **arm.**

109

Bring me the **data** for this case.

The **data** are in that envelope.

acclimate   To become accustomed to.

The only pronunciation was ă klī′mĭt; the second syllable received the accent, and the i was long. Now it may also be pronounced ăk′lĭ māt.

It is difficult for a stranger to become **acclimated** to our weather.

You will soon be **acclimated** to our ways.

aerial   Relating to the air.

Formerly it was necessary to make this a word of four syllables, ā ēr′ĭ ăl. Now it may also be pronounced as a word of three syllables, âr′ĭ ăl.

Our **aerial** forces need to be increased.

Have you put up the **aerial** for your radio?

centenary   One hundred years.

No more is one compelled to accent the first syllable of this word, **cen′te nar′y,** for **cen ten′a ry** is now also correct.

We celebrated the **bicentenary** of his birth in 1933.

Tomorrow will be the **centenary** of his death.

adult   A grown-up person.

Although one often heard this word pronounced **ad′ult,** this pronunciation was not sanctioned by any dictionary until 1934. Now one may accent the first or last syllable of this word and be correct.

Our class is composed of **adults.**

The **adult** population of this city is very large.

abdomen   Part of the body.

To accent the first or the second syllable of this word is now correct.

He complained of a pain in his **abdomen.**

The football player was kicked in the **abdomen.**

romance   Fiction dealing with picturesque and adventurous scenes and incidents; a series of such incidents.

One may now accent the first or the last syllable of this word.

Their **romance** came to a sudden end.

Today there are too many books of **romance.**

discourse (*n.*) A formal speech or composition.

As a noun, this word may be accented on the first or last syllable.

The verb-form must be accented on the last syllable.

This **discourse** was too long.

The professor will now deliver his **discourse** on English.

We shall **discourse** upon that plan tomorrow.

finance   Science of receiving or expending **revenue.** In the plural, the money resource of a state, individual, or the like.

To say fī′năns for the noun is no longer incorrect.

If one accents the first syllable, the i must be long. **Fī năns′** and **fĭ năns′** are also correct.

For the verb, the i may be long or short, but the accent *must* be on the *last* syllable, as **fĭ năns′**; fī nans′.

What has happened to the **finances** of our state?

I shall not **finance** (*v.*) that undertaking.

dictionary   A book that gives the spelling, meaning, and pronunciation of words.

It will surely please every red-blooded American to know that he may now say **dic′tion ar′y** without being corrected. Hitherto, it was necessary to say **dic′tionary**; that is, it was not permissible to place a secondary accent on the third syllable.

The new edition of the **dictionary** has been published.

Try to cultivate the **dictionary** habit.

appreciative   Showing appreciation.

Like the word **dictionary,** this word may now have a secondary accent—**ap pre′ci a′tive.** In this case, the fourth syllable **a** is long, as in **day.** In **ap pre′ci a tive,** the **a** is like the **a** in **sofa** or **ask.**

The audience was very **appreciative.**

Was he **appreciative** of what you did for him?

coadjutor   Helper; assistant.

Many people considered **co ad ju'tor** an affected pronunciation. Still, it was the only correct form. Now, however, one may also say **co ad'ju tor.**

Who will be appointed his **coadjutor?**

With the help of my **coadjutor,** this work will be finished next month.

pretense   A claim or pretension, usually not supported by fact.

This word, which may be spelled **pretense** or **pretence,** may now be accented on the first or last syllable.

He made no **pretense** to study his lesson.

His **pretenses** were soon discovered.

vaudeville   Variety as to stage performances.

No longer is one obliged to pronounce this word as one of two syllables. It may also have three syllables.

Our **vaudeville** theater has closed.

Many men prefer **vaudeville** to the cinema.

dictator   One in whom is invested supreme authority in any line.

No more is one compelled to place the accent on the second syllable (**dic ta'tor**), as **dic'ta tor** is also correct.

That country has a new **dictator.**

He was a veritable **dictator** with his men.

detail (*n.*)   A minute portion; a particular (used chiefly in the plural).

The noun-form of this word may now be accented on the first or last syllable. The verb-form must be accented on the last syllable.

We have not learned the **details** of their scheme.

He explained every **detail** of the new plan.

bouquet   A bunch of flowers.

Formerly it was necessary to have the first syllable rhyme with **flue**; now it may also rhyme with **go.** In either case, the accent must be placed on the last syllable: **bōō kā'; bō kā'.**

The **bouquet** was placed on the desk.

Many **bouquets** were presented to the members of the play.

112

electricity

It is your choice now to make the first syllable ė or ĕl.

There is no **electricity** in our classroom.
Many trains are now run by **electricity.**

harass   To exhaust; to weary by importunity.

To place the accent on the last syllable of **harass** was at one time incorrect. Now it is permissible to accent its first or last syllable.

Do not **harass** me with such questions.
We were **harassed** with debt.

adept (*n.*)   One fully skilled or proficient in anything.

To accent the first or the last syllable of the noun **adept** is now correct.

By diligent work he has become a tennis **adept.**
To be sure, he is an **adept** in the use of words.

conduit   An artificial channel, such as a pipe; a canal.

It was always necessary to pronounce this word as one of two syllables: kŏn′dĭt. Now one may also use three syllables: kŏn′do͞o ĭt.

The **conduits** have been laid.
All **conduits** of learning have been opened for us.

rabies   Dog madness.

One is now correct whether he says rā′bĭ ēz or rā′bēz.

The dog is affected with **rabies.**
An examination revealed that the animal had **rabies.**

TRUE OR FALSE TEST

Ten of the following statements are incorrect. Try to find them and make the necessary corrections.

1. The last syllable of **genuine** never rhymes with **mine**.
2. **Bade** may be pronounced to rhyme with **made**.
3. The sound of the first syllable in **zoology** rhymes with **glue**.
4. **Detour** has more than one correct pronunciation.
5. The second syllable in **lamentable** is accented.
6. The first syllable in **comely** is pronounced **comb**.
7. **Acclimate** has two correct pronunciations.
8. Always accent the first syllable of **hospitable**.
9. The preferred pronunciation of **leisure** is **lĕzh'er**.
10. The first syllable of **faucet** may be pronounced **fas**.
11. Never accent the second syllable of **despicable**.
12. **Quay** is pronounced as though it were spelled **key**.
13. **Dictator** must be accented on the first syllable.
14. The first syllable of **coupon** may be pronounced **Q** or **koo**.
15. In **status** the first syllable should rhyme with **play**.
16. **Conduit** has two recorded pronunciations.
17. **Abdomen** may be pronounced **ab'domen** or **abdo'men**.
18. **Impious** is now accented on the second syllable.
19. It is correct to say **sec'retar'y**.
20. Always accent the last syllable of **adult**.
21. The first syllable of **sinecure** may rhyme with **dine** or **din**.
22. **Conversant** must be accented on the first syllable.
23. There are two recorded pronunciations for **data**.
24. **Pianist** may be accented on the first or second syllable.

Lesson 88

RECASTING EXERCISE (REVIEW)

Rewrite each sentence by using a word from the following list that will convey the original meaning.

Example: He was resolved to let no obstacle stand in his way.
He was resolved to **surmount** every obstacle.

accrue	lenient	ascertain
censure (*v.*)	advocate	temporary
augment	ultimately	dissolution
nominal	surmount	exorbitant
manifest	facility	erroneous
demolish	profound	superfluous

1. Much good will come to you through the study of words.

2. The judge was rather easy with the prisoner.

3. The medicine relieved the pain for only a short time.

4. He did not show any interest in football.

5. The old building was torn down last week.

6. We tried to find out the names of his associates.

7. By hard work he will in time be a success.

8. It is our wish to be able to work easily.

9. They are spreading rumors which are not true.

10. He was called down for his laziness.

11. She did not pay much for her dress.

12. Their business came to an end last year.

13. The taxes in our city are altogether too high.

14. Our aim is to get a good many useful words.

15. That remark was not necessary.

16. Are you in favor of less homework for the students?

17. We have a mighty fine respect for our instructor.

Lesson 89

WORDS OF THE 5,000 POSITION IN THORNDIKE'S LIST

Exercise 1

ascertain	(ă sẽr tān')	**casual**	(kăzh'ủ ȧl)
bewilder	(bẽ wĭl'dẽr)	**subsist**	(sŭb sĭst')
immortal	(ĭm môr'tăl)	**pertain**	(pẽr tān')
merciless	(mẽr'sĭ lĕs)	**innumerable**	(ĭn nū'mẽr ȧ b'l)

Fill the blanks with words from the preceding list:

1. I was _____ by the sea of faces before me.
2. Mr. Currie had made _____ speeches before this one.
3. You are _____ in your criticism of my faults.
4. We are here to _____ the truth of the affair.
5. I was only a _____ observer at the scene.
6. Does your visit _____ to the accident of yesterday?
7. It is useless to try to _____ on such a meager sum.
8. The speech that Patrick Henry made that day is _____.

Exercise 2

humorous	(hūm'ẽr ŭs)	**delusion**	(dẽ lū'zhŭn)
identify	(ī dĕn'tĭ fī)	**indebted**	(ĭn dĕt'ĕd)
ascribe	(ă skrīb')	**torrid**	(tŏr'rĭd)
pinnacle	(pĭn'nă k'l)	**subjection**	(sŭb jĕk'shŭn)

Fill the blanks with words from the preceding list:

1. He had reached the _____ of success before he was forty.
2. I am _____ to you for the privilege of being here.
3. Mr. Bromley's friends were in utter _____ to him.
4. The many _____ sayings of this author have won him a reputation.
5. I shall never forget my feelings on that _____ day.
6. Can you _____ the writing?
7. One could never _____ evil motives to Mrs. Bell.
8. It is a _____ to think we can succeed under such circumstances.

Lesson 90

HISTORICAL TERMS

Each of the words in this list describes, or tells about, some characteristic or act of George Washington, or some event that happened during his career. Endeavor to construct with each word a sentence that will be true to history.

Example: **aide-de-camp.**

As **aide-de-camp** to General Braddock, Colonel Washington won honor for his self-reliance and leadership.

President	disciplinarian	convention
liberty	education	redress
clemency	debate	strategy
humility	advocate (*n.*)	expedients
ambitious	martyr	veracity
burgesses	wilderness	grievance
volunteer	integrity	alienate
preserve	submissive	vigilant
simplicity	prowess	ignominious
ponder	vanquish	hostile
aide-de-camp	critical	ratification
literary	attachment	dualizing
non-importation	temporize	legislature
proposition	paternal	accurate
dismember	countrymen	disloyal
delegate	committee of	draft
loyalty	correspondence	regiment

Exercise

1. Construct sentences containing:

   courteous remonstrances   critical period
   humiliating rejection   stanch advocate
   armed resistance   foreign sympathizers

2. Write a synonym for:

   apathy   indissoluble   inevitable

3. Write an antonym for:

   conciliate   generosity   loyalty

117

ANTONYMS

An antonym is a word which is opposite in meaning to another word in the same language. It is the opposite of a synonym, which means a word having the same meaning as another in the same language.

Word	Antonym	Word	Antonym
past	future	conceal	reveal
truth	error	include	exclude
accept	reject	natural	artificial
absent	present	increase	decrease
success	failure	alien	native
continue	discontinue	positive	negative
inhale	exhale	acquit	convict
united	divided	hostile	friendly
mortal	immortal	traitor	patriot
replace	displace	modern	ancient
collect	distribute	generous	miserly
import	export	flattery	sincerity
awkward	clever	barbarous	civilized
barrier	opening	arrange	derange
attack (v.)	defend	criminal (a.)	lawful
antique	modern	anxiety	calmness
radical	conservative	conscious	insensible
polite	discourteous	admissible	unallowable
alacrity	indolence	purchase (v.)	dispose of
obsolete	novel	addicted	unaccustomed

Exercise

Construct sentences with:

admissible	insensible	alacrity	anxiety

Lesson 92

ANTONYMS AND SYNONYMS

Exercises

A. State whether the boldfaced word in the second column is an antonym or a synonym of the word given in the first column, or select an antonym or a synonym from the two remaining words:

attain	**abandon,** miss, accomplish.
pardon (*n.*)	amnesty, penalty, **retribution.**
dress (*n.*)	**uniform,** array, vestments.
friendly	warlike, tender, **amicable.**
tire (*v.*)	fatigue, refresh, **exhaust.**
fraud	treason, **integrity,** swindle.
attack (*n.*)	invasion, **retreat,** surrender.
victory	success, destruction, **supremacy.**
rest (*n.*)	recreation, **tranquillity,** commotion.
vigilant	**inattentive,** cautious, unwary.
prejudice	bias, **partiality,** unfairness.
catastrophe	**prosperity,** calamity, boon.
esteem (*n.*)	hatred, respect, **aversion.**
poetry	poesy, **prose,** verse.
faith	trust, disbelief, **confidence.**
afraid	timid, fearless, **terrified.**
injury	damage, remedy, **injustice.**
patience	**fortitude,** anger, leniency.
renounce	disclaim, uphold, **vindicate.**
repentance	sorrow, approval, **compunction.**

B. Write sentences containing:

supremacy	tranquillity	compunction
vigilance	prejudice	catastrophe

C. Explain these phrases:

fraudulent act	prejudicial remark
pardonable pride	endless patience

119

Lesson 93

ANTONYMS

Matching Exercise

Select from Group II the antonyms of the words in Group I. Match them—that is, write the word on the same line with its antonym.

Group I

praise	gloomy	feeble
uncertain	knowledge	abundance
adopt	seldom	collect
export	unkind	inferior

Group II

jovial	robust	reject
scatter	censure	import
positive	superior	charitable
often	scarcity	ignorance

Words Illustrated in Sentences

The meanings of some of the preceding words may be obtained from these sentences:

1. The teacher possessed a **jovial** spirit.
2. The principal did not **censure** him for his many mistakes.
3. There was a decided **scarcity** of sugar during the World War.
4. It pays to be **charitable** to your fellow students.

Antonyms

healthy	Frail, weak, delicate.
endure	Despair, succumb, break down.
rise (*v.*)	Descend, sink, decline.
permission	Refusal, denial, opposition.
perfect (*adj.*)	Corrupt, faulty, defective.
union	Division, separation, dissociation.
pardon (*v.*)	Convict, condemn, sentence.
care (*n.*)	Disregard, negligence, indifference.

Questions

1. What is the difference between **healthy** and **healthful?**
2. Use **perfect** as an adjective; as a verb.

ANTONYMS

A person who wishes to possess an effective vocabulary should have at his ready disposal a copious supply of both synonyms and antonyms. Here are some common examples of antonyms:

Word	Antonym	Word	Antonym
barren	fertile	simple	intricate
jovial	gloomy	constant	variable
feeble	robust	rigid	pliant
expand	contract	indolent	diligent
sincere	deceitful	real	fictitious
repellent	attractive	obscure	clear
knowledge	ignorance	strength	weakness
sullen	cheerful	interior	exterior
superior	inferior	frugal	extravagant
worldly	spiritual	adopt	reject
definite	vague	restore	remove
severe	lenient	radical	conservative

Exercise

Fill each blank with the correct form of the word found in parentheses:

1. The crop was very large on account of the (fertile) _____ of the soil.
2. The governor refused to show any (lenient) _____ to the prisoner.
3. *Materiality* and (spiritual) _____ are words directly opposed to each other.
4. What is the (contract) _____ for "could not"?
5. People are reading too much (fictitious) _____.
6. The pupil was rebuked for his (indolent) _____.
7. (Constant) _____ of purpose is a characteristic of great men.
8. One should at all times practice (frugal) _____.
9. Washington did not attack because of his (inferior) _____ in numbers.
10. That business has undergone great (expand) _____.
11. Have you mastered the (intricate) _____ of your machine?

121

TEST VII

(This test embraces material found in Lessons 83–93 inclusive.)

I. Write sentences containing:

inveigle	disputable	impious	strategic
requited	harass	impotent	lamentable

II. Give words that conform with these definitions:

1. Easily bent.
2. Disfigured.
3. To take unjustly or by force.
4. Face to face.
5. At the same time.
6. Prolonged life.
7. Not to be compared.
8. Sharp, severe.

III. Fill each blank with a word taken from this list:

clemency	humility	changeable
reduction	cherished	imperative

1. The judge thought it was _____ for him to show _____ to the prisoner.
2. The laborers _____ the idea that there would be no _____ of wages.
3. Jefferson's _____ was known by everyone.
4. New England is noted for its _____ weather.

IV. Write an antonym for:

success	obsolete	mortal	accept

V. Give a synonym for:

friendly	vigilant	renounce	attain

VI. Let these adjectives qualify nouns; as, **superior officer**:

1. repellent
2. lenient
3. judicial
4. rebellious
5. accurate
6. submissive

VII. What is the noun-form of each word?

severe	sincere	fictitious
constant	admissible	distribute

VIII. Give the verb-form of:

summary	imaginary	criticism
adoption	rebellion	concession

Lesson 95

WORDS OF THE 4,000–5,000 POSITION
IN THORNDIKE'S LIST

arouse	blunder	respective	attendance
comply	intimate	insurance	continuous
avenge	marshal	asunder	refreshment
launch	bramble	lonesome	tenderness
beseech	compound	interview	brightness
costume	journal	converse	resolution
invest	livery	genuine	proposition
awaken	mellow	fragment	captivity
lavish	resound	attribute	sanctify
mumble	villain	gladness	banishment
manly	servile	bulletin	contribute
besiege	tenant	courtesy	respectful
legend	reprove	assistant	atmosphere
deign	warfare	glorify	sandwich
revel	scramble	conclusion	catalogue
bewail	agreement	scornful	sentiment
defile	revolve	testify	organization
replace	almighty	federal	communicate
scour	serene	idolatry	successive
ruffle	apparel	imperfect	withstand
vital	response	partake	curiosity
scanty	syllable	rebellion	anniversary
vivid	camera	pioneer	separation
scorch	remorse	salvation	legislature
shrewd	fraction	sovereign	demonstration

Exercise

1. Use these words in sentences:

captivity	asunder	communicate
curiosity	scornful	banishment

2. Let these adjectives modify nouns:

responsive	fragmentary	conclusive
fractional	remorseful	atmospheric

123

Lesson 96

SYNONYMS

A list of synonyms of common words follows:

order (*n.*)	mandate	command	direction
heretic	renegade	pervert	dissenter
important	momentous	decisive	weighty
arrange	classify	adjust	assort
hide	suppress	mask	disguise
catch	apprehend	seize	capture
home	residence	abode	dwelling
cease	discontinue	desist	refrain
promote	foster	further	assist
difficult	laborious	hard	arduous
honest	honorable	frank	sincere
change (*v.*)	transform	alter	vary
teach	educate	inform	instruct
victory	supremacy	success	conquest
fear	timidity	dread	fright
pray	beseech	entreat	invoke

Exercise

1. Write three words that are built upon the root **vert,** such as, for example, **pervert;** two, on **sist,** such as **desist.**

2. What is the noun-form of each of the following?

     arduous   **apprehend**   **classify**

3. Consult the dictionary for the difference between **further** and **farther.**

4. Give two words that are related to:

     educate   **inform**   **decisive**

5. Use in sentences:

     timidity   **instruct**   **supremacy**

6. To which words of the above list are these related?

heresy	suppression	dissension	seizable
sincerity	timorous	captivate	adjustable

124

Lesson 97

SYNONYMS

pardon	forgive	acquit	absolve
surrender	relinquish	yield	abandon
wealth	affluence	fortune	opulence
hatred	animosity	dislike	hostility
mourn	lament	regret	deplore
pain	suffering	ache	anguish
healthy	wholesome	sound	vigorous
support	maintain	bear	uphold
attack (*v.*)	encounter	assail	besiege
complain	remonstrate	growl	grumble
pay (*n.*)	allowance	salary	wages
hazard	jeopardy	risk	danger
attain	accomplish	secure	achieve
faithful	trustworthy	loyal	devoted
journey	excursion	tour	trip
behavior	deportment	conduct	manners

Exercise

Give a synonym, in addition to those found on this page, for each of the bold-type words.

1. He refused to **relinquish** his claim to the throne.
2. All **animosity** should be wiped out of our minds.
3. A **vigorous** attempt to take the fort was made.
4. **Opulence** does not always indicate greatness.
5. The principal **remonstrated** with the student for his inactivity and laziness.
6. To go out in this blizzard would be placing one's life in **jeopardy.**
7. Mr. Pronovost **achieved** great distinction as a writer.
8. The woman's heart was filled with **anguish** on account of her son's trouble.

MISCELLANEOUS WORDS WITH EXERCISES

grope	To feel one's way; to seek blindly.
conspire	To plot together.
injustice	Wrong; injury; unfairness.
historic	Associated with, or famous in, history.
recollect	To remember; to recall; to call to mind.
interfere	To collide; to clash; to come between.
selection	State of being chosen; a choice.
lawless	Not restrained by law; unruly.
gorge (v.)	To swallow greedily or in large mouthfuls.
frightful	Terrifying; exciting fear.
impious	Irreligious; wicked; profane.
definite	Precise; exact; having fixed limits.
flatterer	One who pleases by compliments.
situation	Locality; condition.
horizontal	Pertaining to, or parallel to, the horizon.
confirmation	Proof; convincing testimony.

Exercise

Fill each blank with a word from the list above:

1. I cannot give you a _____ answer before tomorrow.
2. The _____ judge was forced to resign.
3. One should never _____ himself with food.
4. She made a _____ from the merchandise sent by the store.
5. A committee was sent to receive a _____ of the report.
6. Do you think we would _____ against our benefactors?
7. We visited the _____ grounds at Williamsburg.

True or False Test

Horizontal is an antonym for parallel.

Impious is pronounced im pī'ous.

Gorge may also be used as a noun.

Conspire, aspire, and inspire come from the same Latin root.

126

SYNONYMS

precedent	example	case	instance
humane	kindhearted	gentle	charitable
impudence	insolence	boldness	rudeness
difference	discrepancy	variety	contrast
do	accomplish	realize	perform
clever	ingenious	able	skillful
hinder	interrupt	deter	retard
agreeable	contented	cheerful	pleasant
model	imitation	pattern	example
baffle	frustrate	foil	thwart
contract (n.)	agreement	pledge	promise
modesty	bashfulness	reserve	shyness
apportion	distribute	allot	grant
esteem (v.)	consider	regard	value
innocent	faultless	clean	upright
transact	negotiate	perform	accomplish

Some of the words from the preceding list are here used in sentences:

1. An attempt was made to **thwart** his plans.
2. The teacher could not tolerate his **insolence**.
3. His faultless life served as a **model** to thousands of young men.
4. I shall **apportion** the shares equally among the five children.
5. Mr. Jones was downhearted because his plans were **frustrated**.
6. He **esteemed** it an honor to be able to address such a learned gathering.

Exercise

1. Construct sentences including:

    frustrated plans   gross discrepancy
    established precedent   charitable intention

2. What is the noun-form of **ingenious**?
3. Give the adjective-form of **insolence**.

127

Lesson 100

SYNONYMS

carry	remove	bring	take
revolution	insurrection	riot	revolt
entrance	admittance	approach	access
purchase	procure	buy	obtain
evident	apparent	clear	manifest
high	elevated	lofty	towering
praise	compliment	acclaim	applause
succeed	thrive	win	prosper
restrain	suppress	hinder	check
mercy	forgiveness	pity	kindness
vacant	unoccupied	empty	unfilled
normal	ordinary	regular	usual
check	repress	stop	impede
education	instruction	culture	learning
help	befriend	support	assist
old	venerable	aged	ancient

Some words from the preceding list are here used in sentences:

1. I could not **restrain** myself from fighting.
2. Everyone was denied **admittance** to the building.
3. The presidency of the firm is an **elevated** position for Mr. Brophy.
4. Lincoln's **towering** physique attracted the attention of everyone.
5. Soldiers were sent to put an end to the **insurrection.**

Exercise

Select the correct form of the word in parentheses:

1. (**Manifest**) _____ he is guilty.
2. The soldiers practically (**venerable**) _____ General Wayne.
3. Our city has made great strides in the (**education**) _____ field.
4. Thomas found the lesson very (**instruction**) _____.

Lesson 101

CORRECT USE OF WORDS

Exercise

In each of these sentences, tell whether the word in parentheses is the proper one to use, or whether there is one more appropriate. If a substitute is preferred or required, state what it should be.

1. Was he (**conscious**) of his ignorance?
2. The man's (**character**) for contributing to charitable causes was universally known.
3. The student displayed a great (**desire**) for mathematical work.
4. Although the law (**prohibited**) the sale of intoxicants, it did not (**prohibit**) people from engaging in that business.
5. Mr. Smith's (**frugality**) in not properly feeding and clothing his children was brought to the attention of the civil authorities.
6. The United States and Canada have many (**mutual**) obligations.
7. The marks of the struggle were (**evident**) in the broken shrubbery and trampled ground.

Questions

1. Which is more lasting, **compunction** or **repentance?**
2. Is **pernicious** a stronger word than **injurious,** inasmuch as it refers to the power to destroy or kill?
3. In what way does a **discourse** differ from a **speech?**
4. Is it a **spy** or a **scout** who enters in disguise within the enemy's lines?
5. Does a mother **felicitate** or **congratulate** her son upon his promotion?
6. In speaking of an American going to live in Europe, would one say he **immigrates** or **emigrates** from this country?
7. How does **imminent** differ from **threatening?**
8. Is **unconscious** the same as **subconscious?**
9. What is the pronunciation of each of the following?

column   victuals   sesame

Lesson 102

SYNONYMOUS SUBSTITUTIONS

Exercise 1

A. In place of the bold-type word or words in these sentences, use one from the following list that will render the same meaning:

mantel   pendent   extent   mantle   extant   pendant

1. A diamond-studded **ornament** was her Christmas present.
2. His works are no longer **in existence**.
3. He placed the clock on the **chimney piece**.
4. To what **length** he pursued his victim I do not know.
5. I threw the **cloak** over my shoulders to keep warm.
6. **Hanging** from the ceiling was the mistletoe.

B. Pupils who contemplate entering the business or clerical field after graduation should be prepared to meet the following words. A knowledge both of the spelling and of the meaning of each word should be possessed by all pupils.

Place each word in a sentence:

retail	acknowledgment	bonus
reserve	employee	draft
payable	attachment	assets
indorse	dividends	deficit

Questions

1. **Retail** may be accented on the first syllable or on the second syllable. How is the meaning affected by the accent?
2. State the difference between **employee** and **employer**.
3. Is there another spelling for **indorse**?
4. What is the correct pronunciation of **clientele**?

Exercise 2

Fill each blank with a word from the list above:

1. Kindly _____ this check for me.
2. The bank has a large _____ fund.
3. Consider this message an _____ of your letter.

130

WORDS OFTEN CONFUSED

elicit	disease	immigrant
illicit	deceased	emigrant
prophecy (—sē)	counsel	statute
prophesy (—sī)	council	stature

The distinction between these words is illustrated by their use in the following sentences:

1. Prohibition made the sale of intoxicating liquors **illicit.**
2. The judge could not **elicit** from the convict any information as to who killed the jailer.
3. The old woman's **prophecy,** that there would be a great war, was fulfilled.
4. Did the baseball coach **prophesy** a victory for his team?
5. The aged man is suffering from a lingering **disease.**
6. The relatives of the **deceased** gathered to hear the reading of the will.
7. Attorney Skehan was the **counsel** for the man accused of burning the barn.
8. The students wisely accepted the good **counsel** given them by their principal.
9. The members of the aldermanic **council** voted to grant more money for educational purposes.
10. Nearly every **immigrant** to this country desires to learn the English language.
11. The number of **emigrants** from the United States to Italy during the past year was very small.
12. There is a new state **statute** that will abolish poor headlights on automobiles.
13. That boy's **stature** was a sure proof that he would make a good football player.

Exercise

Select the proper word:

1. (**Elicit, illicit**) means to draw out.
2. An adviser is called a (**councilor, counselor**).

Lesson 104

WORDS OF THE 5,000–5,500 POSITION IN THORNDIKE'S LIST

abyss	wrestle	consecrate	compassion
chafe	bondage	academy	breathless
bleak	fathom	merciful	hemisphere
allied	cashier	alternate	competition
retail	auction	silvery	astonishment
sieve	marine	blameless	acceptance
allure	blacken	schedule	abominable
pier	urgent	nursery	holiness
taint	pension	camphor	assortment
applaud	weaver	promote	carburetor
vent	bouquet	hosiery	regulation
census	pitiful	capital	confirmation
blouse	altitude	betrothed	bitterness
usurp	faucet	tonnage	chastisement
assent	bulwark	shapeless	attainment
breach	session	precede	investigate
poise	phantom	cardinal	patriotic
wade	woeful	pitiless	conflagration
ascent	finance	noiseless	persecution
muscle	proverb	chivalry	vouchsafe
wintry	forgery	glimmer	deliverer
chide	gossip	heartily	conscientious
asylum	honesty	clearness	visitation
fiction	clergy	courageous	nomination

Exercise

Select the proper definition of each word:

1. Precede means (to go before; to exempt; to follow).
2. To dedicate is (to yield; to give; to consecrate).
3. A synonym for usurp is (owe; seize; use).

Lesson 105

WORDS OFTEN CONFUSED

There are few words in the English language whose meanings are identical. Note the differences existing between the meanings of the following pairs:

ignorant	Not informed.
illiterate	Uneducated, unable to read or write.
conscious	Pertaining to the mind.
aware	Pertaining to what is going on outside of the mind.
majority	More than half.
plurality	More votes than gained by the next highest candidate.
notorious	Well known in an unfavorable sense.
famous	Well known in a favorable sense.
oral	Uttered by the mouth, spoken.
verbal	Expressed in words, whether spoken or written.
compare	To examine so as to show likeness or unlikeness.
contrast (*v.*)	To show the differences.
envious	Desiring or resenting the good fortune of another.
jealous	Suspicious that another desires what is one's own.
plausible	Having the appearance of truth.
feasible	Capable of being done.

If the boldfaced words are not properly employed, make the necessary corrections:

1. His plan for stopping the overflow of water proved **plausible.**

2. Was the contract **oral** or **verbal**?

3. In the senatorial race, Nolan received 63,500 votes, Burns, 52,000 votes, and Brown, 36,500. Nolan won by a **majority** of 11,500.

4. The author has received much **notoriety** from the press because of the valuable books he has written.

5. **Compare** the Wilson administration with that of Coolidge

6. He was **conscious** that he was catching a severe cold.

7. The most **feasible** thing for him to do was to confess his guilt.

8. He is **jealous** of my wealth.

133

Lesson 106

WORD-PAIRS

Exercise 1

A. Fill each blank with one of the following words:

affect	want	envious	let
effect	wish	jealous	leave

1. My admiration of her flowers made her _____.
2. Jones failed to _____ a new plan at the last meeting.
3. His speech did not _____ me as it did you.
4. The two countries were unable to _____ a compromise.
5. I wish you would _____ me do that work.
6. He failed in business for _____ of money.
7. The silver trophy drew _____ glances to the winner.
8. Kindly _____ me, as I have many things to do.

B. Use these words in sentences:

knowledge	advertisement	repetition
monopoly	despicable	cessation
opposition	refutable	remedial
collection	maintenance	isolation

Caution

Care should be taken in regard to the pronunciations of **despicable, refutable,** and **advertisement,** as well as with the spelling of **maintenance.**

Exercise 2

How is each boldfaced word related to a word in the list above?

1. They found it difficult to **refute** our arguments.
2. One should not **isolate** himself from society.
3. An attempt has been made to **monopolize** the steel business.
4. Whom did Tom **oppose** for the captaincy?
5. The teacher could not **maintain** order in the classroom.
6. Let me **repeat** the **remedy.**

134

Lesson 107

ACCENTS

A change of accent affects the meanings and parts of speech of certain words.

Exercise

A. Fill each blank with the correct word, to be selected from this list, and accent the word chosen:

desert   **invalid**   **concert**   **frequent**

1. One should never _____ places where vice exists.
2. The teacher informed him that it was an _____ excuse for his absence.
3. The fall made him an _____ for life.
4. Water is scarce on a _____.
5. I made _____ trips to New York during the year.
6. A loyal man will never _____ his friend.
7. If we _____ our efforts upon this project, we shall succeed.

B. How should the bold-type words be accented? Consult your dictionary for the answers.

1. Our **exports** last year far surpassed our **imports.**
2. The author has made slow **progress** with his book.
3. The next order was, "**Present** arms!"
4. I hope your plan will **progress** as rapidly as possible.
5. We are not **content** with our present wages.
6. There was a great **protest** against the use of firecrackers.
7. I just devoured the **contents** of that book.
8. Are you sure your proposition will not **conflict** with mine?
9. He would not **essay** to undertake the work.
10. Did Mr. Kennedy **address** the student body this week?
11. The police captured two drug **addicts.**
12. We were **subjected** to the third degree.
13. To what **address** shall I send this book?
14. He was so **addicted** to drink that he failed in business.
15. Honor is the **subject** of my story.
16. Dr. Brennan **discoursed** upon the proper form of diet.
17. We have just listened to a **discourse** upon "The Life of Pasteur."

135

Lesson 108

SYNONYMOUS WORDS DISTINGUISHED

Note the distinctions in the use of these words:

We **cease** talking.
We **leave off** work.

We **lead** a blind man.
We **guide** a traveler.

We **choose** one **from** another.
We **prefer** one **to** another.

We **discover** what before existed.
We **invent** what did not exist before.

We **return** what we have borrowed.
We **restore** what we have taken.
We **surrender** what is ours by right.

We **sympathize** with the afflicted.
We **pity** the distressed.
We have **compassion** on the miserable.

We **remunerate** for services received.
We **compensate** for injury or loss.

We **comprehend** what we fully understand.
We **apprehend** what we do not fully comprehend, such as eternity and the infinite.

An **impediment** hinders progress.
An **obstacle** prevents progress.

Emulation is for equality.
Competition is for superiority.

Impracticable means not possible according to the circumstances.
Impossible means not possible according to its nature.

Questions

1. Does **sympathy** differ from **compassion?**
2. How does **ambition** compare with **aspiration?**
3. Can you give two meanings for **apprehend?**

Lesson 109

THE SAME WORDS WITH DIFFERENT ACCENTS

convict (kŏn'vĭkt) (*n.*) The **convict** escaped from the jail.

(kŏn vĭkt') (*v.*) He will surely be **convicted** for stealing the automobile.

rebel (rĕb'ĕl) (*n.*) The **rebel** was put to death.

(rĕ bĕl') (*v.*) One should not **rebel** against the laws of his country.

refuse (rĕf'ūs) (*n.*) The yard was full of **refuse**.

(rĕ fūz') (*v.*) Did the pupil **refuse** to attend the show?

conduct (kŏn'dŭkt) (*n.*) His **conduct** in school was satisfactory.

(kŏn dŭkt') (*v.*) I shall now **conduct** you through our chemistry laboratory.

extract (ĕks'trăkt) (*n.*) Kindly give me that bottle of vanilla **extract**.

(ĕks trăkt') (*v.*) One should try to **extract** much happiness from life.

desert (dĕz'ẽrt) (*n.*) Water is scarce on a **desert**.

(dĕ zẽrt') (*v.*) A true friend will never **desert** his comrades.

concert (kŏn'sẽrt) (*n.*) The band **concert** will commence at 8 P.M.

(kŏn sẽrt') (*v.*) Let us **concert** our efforts toward accomplishing this result.

absent (ăb'sĕnt) (*adj.*) John was **absent** from school yesterday.

(ăb sĕnt') (*v.*) Why did you **absent** yourself from the meeting?

invalid (ĭn'văl ĭd) (*n.*) The **invalid** could not walk without the aid of crutches.

(ĭn văl'ĭd) (*adj.*) When both parties violated certain agreements, the contract was rendered **invalid**.

gallant (găl'lănt) (*adj.*) The **gallant** soldier was decorated for his bravery.

(găl lănt') (*adj.*) He was **gallant** in the presence of ladies.

Exercise

Construct sentences including these words:

wave	symbol	canvas	divers
waive	cymbal	canvass	diverse

WORDS WHOSE MEANINGS ARE OFTEN CONFUSED

Word	Meaning	Example
propose	To offer to do something.	Who will **propose** the new bill?
purpose (*n.*)	Aim; intention.	My **purpose** is clear.
famous	Known in a favorable sense.	Many **famous** people are in this gathering.
notorious	Known in an unfavorable sense.	His name was **notorious.**
majority	More than half.	A **majority** of the committee voted for the measure.
plurality	More than the next highest.	Our candidate won by a large **plurality.**
invent	To produce for the first time.	I wish someone would **invent** a new way of doing this work.
discover	To find something previously known.	We were unable to **discover** any trace of the travelers.
character	Nature, what you are.	He was a man of sterling **character.**
reputation	General opinion.	Your **reputation** is an enviable one.
evidence	Proof.	There was no **evidence** of guilt in his answers.
testimony	Affirmation.	The **testimony** of the witness was favorable to the prisoner.
lightning	Electric discharge in the sky.	The **lightning** was sharp.
lightening	Making lighter.	His thought was of **lightening** the burdens of others.
compare	To examine; to show likeness or unlikeness.	Let us **compare** the two characters.
contrast	To compare; to show unlikeness.	**Contrast** the forces of the Colonists and the British during the Revolution.

Purpose may be used as a verb.

Explain the difference between **majority** and **plurality.**

Lesson 111

MISCELLANEOUS WORDS WITH COMPLETION
EXERCISES

Exercise 1

imperative	Necessary; obligatory.	**studious**	Earnest; attentive.
willful	Intentional; obstinate.	**apprehend**	To understand; to seize.
recoil	To start back in dismay.	**romantic**	Fanciful; improbable.
aggravate	To make worse.	**tranquillity**	Quiet; calmness.

Fill the blanks with appropriate words taken from the list above.

1. My mind _____ at the thought of the horrible deed.
2. His going out of doors tended to _____ his sickness.
3. The father praised his son for his _____ endeavor to remain at the head of his class.
4. The prisoner was accused by the judge of _____ murder.
5. The principal found it _____ to discontinue school dances.
6. It was easy to _____ the cause of his failure.
7. When the war was over, everyone settled down to a period of peace and _____.
8. The author was full of _____ ideas.

Exercise 2

amicable	Friendly; kindly.	**indignant**	Angry.
comment	To speak about.	**vacancy**	Empty space or position.
movable	Capable of being moved.	**animate**	To enliven; rouse.
upbraid	To scold; to call down.	**faulty**	Imperfect; defective.

Fill the blanks in the sentences with words from the preceding list.

1. There will be a _____ in our ranks next month.
2. Everything _____ was taken from the room to allow the young folks more space in which to dance.
3. The _____ teacher _____ the pupil for his lack of manners.
4. The fire-chief _____ upon the _____ construction of the theater.
5. _____ relations exist today between the two countries.

139

Lesson 112

COMPOUND WORDS

A compound word is one made up of two or more simple words.

No rules can be given relative to the use of the hyphen. Many formerly hyphenated words are now being written without the hyphen.

Let us review here some cases in which the hyphen is used:

1. When a numeral adjective precedes **rate**.

2. When adjective expressions are compounded.

3. When **ex** precedes titles.

4. In numbers below one hundred, when these are written out.

5. When fractions are expressed in words and used as adjectives.

Examples are:

first-rate	fifty-six	made-to-order
wild-eyed	good-for-nothing	well-bred
light-haired	ex-president	ill-gotten
four-fifths	good-natured	bad-tempered
stiff-necked	well-known	ex-mayor
by-laws	good-by	loose-tongued
first-class	twenty-nine	court-martial
long-lived	knight-errant	forget-me-not
son-in-law	lookers-on	tête-à-tête

These words, which were at one time compounded, are now written as single words:

welfare	although	already	fulfill
altogether	almighty	artful	inasmuch
hateful	namesake	pastime	notwithstanding

TEST VIII

(This test embraces material found in Lessons 94–111, inclusive.)

I. Give the meaning of:

eligible	provident	irrevocable
precedent	respective	supremacy
restrain	timidity	apprehend

II. Select the proper word:

1. The joke did not (**elicit, illicit**) a smile from him.
2. An (**ignorant, illiterate**) person is one who is unable to read or write.
3. People who come to this country are called (**emigrants, immigrants**).
4. Do you (**purpose, propose**) calling on Mr. Condon this afternoon?

III. Explain the difference between:

majority	and	plurality
plausible	and	feasible
confuse	and	confound
reputation	and	character

IV. Which of these words should be hyphenated?

altogether	dining room	twenty two
longlived	son in law	good by

V. Construct sentences containing:

dauntless spirit	contemptible act
manifest purpose	slight discrepancy
adroit flatterer	decisive victory

VI. How does a change of accent affect these words?

refuse	frequent	invalid
extract	conduct	concert

VII. Explain the difference between these word-pairs:

comprehend	invent	obstacle
apprehend	discover	impediment

141

Lesson 113

HYPHENATED COMPOUNDS

Can you find six words in this list that should not be hyphenated?

able-bodied	vice-president
meat-market	absent-minded
four-wheeled	assembly-room
clear-headed	feeble-minded
eye-minded	fifty-seven
old-fashioned	book-learning
good-natured	post-mortem
middle-sized	tailor-made
self-respect	up-to-date
long-lived	world-wide
second-rate	half-hearted
candle-power	law-abiding
left-handed	safe-deposit
ex-president	sober-minded
machine-made	open-mouthed
well-known	mother-in-law
uncalled-for	self-confidence
half-mast	poverty-stricken
four-in-hand	long-suffering
trade-mark	noble-minded
week-end	ready-made
sure-footed	high-priced

Exercise

1. Use in sentences:

half-hearted attempt	good-natured criticism
open-mouthed surprise	uncalled-for rebuke
long-suffering patience	world-wide recognition

2. Write two words which are related to **confidence.**

3. From what verb is **stricken** derived?

142

Lesson 114

COMPOUND WORDS

Study these words, which illustrate the approved usage in compounds:

Solid Compounds

eyeglass	flaxseed	jawbone
juryman	anybody	network
beefsteak	bookstore	barnyard
barefoot	outside	pocketbook
headstrong	roadway	ballroom
earthquake	homesick	switchboard
greenback	ferryboat	bathroom
bedroom	firearms	stockholder
snowfall	horseback	subdivision
pineapple	cardboard	commonplace
keynote	storeroom	tablecloth
postmark	yearbook	timekeeper
typewriter	overhead	warehouse
barbershop	bellboy	clearinghouse

Two-Word Combinations

half dollar	railroad company
fellow citizen	major general
plate glass	profit sharing
train shed	life insurance
grass seed	good morning
dress goods	ocean steamer
coal fields	common sense
alarm clock	safety valve
cast iron	parcel post
ballot box	ticket office
income tax	assembly room
fire escape	all right
apple pie	assistant director

Lesson 115

MISCELLANEOUS WORDS WITH DEFINITIONS AND EXERCISE

demolish	To throw down; to destroy.
indolent	Avoiding labor; lazy.
exposure	The revelation of; the being open to attack.
animosity	Hostility; hatred; enmity.
compulsion	Force; obligation; restraint.
defenseless	Without protection or defense.
influential	Having, or exerting, power.
seasonable	Occurring in good, or proper, time.
aggressive	Moving forward with vigor; disposed to attack things.
expressive	Serving to represent vividly; indicative.
wearisome	Causing exhaustion; tedious.
sensational	Exciting great interest.
venomous	Full of poison; spiteful.
admonition	Friendly reproof or warning.
irritable	Easily provoked to anger; sensitive.
extravagance	Excess in anything; waste.

Exercise

1. Use in sentences:

indolent pupil	feeling of animosity
aggressive means	venomous attack
irritable mood	spirit of compulsion
expressive English	word of admonition

2. What is the noun-form of **venomous**? What is the verb-form of **admonition**?

3. What is the adjective-form of **extravagance**?

4. Construct sentences with:

compulsory	aggression	defensive
influence (*v.*)	irritation	sensation

144

Lesson 116

GILMARTIN'S FIFTY SPELLING HAZARDS

This list of advanced words has been given by the author to many students and to many professional people. He has rarely received a perfect paper.

pique	reveille
abscess	embarrass
kimono	cemetery
rarefy	prophesy (*v.*)
harass	ecstasy
parallel	gauging
symmetry	decadence
abeyance	bacillus
allotted	accommodate
cynical	complacence
privilege	inoculate
amethyst	accessible
assassin	defendant
asphyxiate	obscene
changeable	acquiesce
pyorrhea	ingenious
mien	relevant
sluice (slōōs)	irresistible
feasible	battalion
languor	questionnaire
massacre	diphtheria
occurrence	anonymous
mucilage	poinsettia
heinous	sarsaparilla
accumulate	transcendent

Exercise

Give two pronunciations for:

harass   reveille

145

Lesson 117

DICTIONARY WORK

Many pupils enter high school with an imperfect knowledge of dictionary usage. This defect should be remedied as quickly as possible. One or two lessons of an intensive nature will procure satisfactory results.

Exercise

A. Arrange these words in dictionary fashion, that is, alphabetize them, and give their accents and meanings:

defection	deference	dairying
deflection	deduction	description
decree	dauntless	discriminate
dangerous	dandelion	disappear
discomfort	disorganize	dislocate
dictation	describable	degradation

B. Derive the meaning of each bold-type word from its use in the sentence:

1. The President said he wished at least a week in which to **deliberate** on the matter.
2. All **inflammable** substances, such as gasoline and kerosene, were removed from the building.
3. His conduct proved that he lacked the **rudiments** of good breeding.
4. The father was killed, and in a short time the family was reduced to **indigence.**
5. One should never **isolate** himself from his friends.
6. The judge was noted for his **severity.**
7. Smith was not **authorized** to sell the property.

C. What is the verb-form of each?

deference   **deduction**   **degradation**

D. Construct sentences with:

dauntless spirit   indescribable suffering
slight defection   discriminating act

146

Lesson 118

SPELLING CONTEST RESULTS

The following lists, reported from national spelling contests, may profitably be studied as important examples of words commonly misspelled. The first list contains words which were incorrectly spelled at the preliminaries of the Naugatuck Valley Spelling Contest, in Connecticut. Only one chance was given to the oral spellers.

rabid	gallantry	fashionable
corpse	possibility	cinnamon
similar	mischievous	encouragement
deferred	musician	appropriating
cipher	obsequies	defendants
papal	intimate	adjournment
seize	scarcely	interfering
abscess	precedence	obsequious

Words missed at the final Naugatuck Valley contest:

ably	allotted	colossal
tying	feasible	cynical
suffice	corridor	vigilance
seize	monstrous	abeyance
valleys	arduous	stimulus

Words missed in the National Finals at Washington, D. C.:

bacillus	adhesive	precarious
quiz	amethyst	approbation
epitaph	esophagus	decadence
knack	complacence	baccalaureate

Some words missed in other National Finals were:

onerous	correlate	cogitation
prodigious	dilatory	ingratiate
monastery	separative	imminent
adequate	diaphanous	catastrophe

Lesson 119

WORDS AND THEIR DEFINITIONS

Matching Exercises

A. State, according to number, which of the definitions below match these words:

Words

1. contraband   4. fraudulent   7. justify
2. eject   5. abrogate   8. sagacity
3. integrity   6. imperative   9. pillage

Definitions

1. To repeal; to abolish.   4. To expel.
2. To warrant.   5. Expressive of a command.
3. Forbidden trade.   6. Keen judgment.
7. Honesty, uprightness.
8. To plunder.
9. Deceitful, dishonest.

B. Select from Group 2 a synonym for each word in Group 1:

Group 1

honesty	disease	eldest
rustic	laughable	yearly
alarmed	exact	permit
polite	increase	satisfied

Group 2

sickness	integrity	rural
annually	frightened	expand
ludicrous	allow	accurate
courteous	contented	oldest

Completion Exercise

Fill each blank with a word taken from Group 2:

1. We should always be _____ to our superiors.
2. The _____ of Washington was never questioned.
3. Her attempt to look young proved very _____.

148

Lesson 120

REVIEW QUESTIONS

1. Is **aggravate** used properly in this sentence?

The actions of that boy **aggravate** me.

2. Can you give two plural forms for **brother** and distinguish between their meanings?

3. Which word, **stationery** or **stationary**, means fixed and permanent?

4. Are **remonstrate** and **demonstrate** both accented on the first syllable?

5. Which is the American, and which the English, spelling for these words?

center   centre   theater   theatre

6. State which word or words are accented incorrectly.

com bat′	a dult′	ad dress′
fi nance′	des′pic a ble	hos pit′a ble
pre tense′	di lute′	com′par a ble

7. What is the general spelling rule for **ie** and **ei** when they are pronounced like ē?

8. What is wrong with each sentence?

a. His council endeavored to affect a satisfactory settlement.
b. We found Miami a very healthy place.

9. Can you find three misspelled words in these sentences?

a. We shall establish a bad preceedent if we permit Mr. Brown to supercede the present chairman.
b. I did not approve of such proceedure.
c. He is mischievous, but not bad.

10. Should **dining room** be spelled with a hyphen?

11. How do you form the plural of letters of the alphabet and numbers?

WORDS OF THE 5,500–6,000 POSITION
IN THORNDIKE'S LIST

absorb	frailty	heritage	accordance
extol	hideous	blaspheme	conspicuous
baffle	adverse	federation	repentance
faulty	faithless	hesitate	boisterous
absurd	moisten	contention	accusation
chaos	subside	aeroplane	immigrant
broil	alcohol	mortgage	co-operative
fabric	visage	civilize	subjection
adult	chemical	venerable	adventurous
crochet	fitness	alliance	cathedral
bias	antique	prostrate	missionary
critic	fortify	cowardice	compliment
aerial	boldness	ingredient	allowance
compete	suffrage	apparatus	capacious
bomb	creditor	tremulous	ridiculous
cipher	fixture	blasphemy	alteration
alert	hostile	peaceable	insignificant
brutal	sprightly	unbelief	charitable
debtor	flounder	architect	immortality
allay	trivial	senseless	appreciation
civic	strangle	particle	concession
fickle	premium	structure	forbearance
allege	oriental	pilgrimage	appropriate
impair	postscript	tapestry	preliminary
annex	ointment	subsequent	demonstrative

Exercise

1. Use these phrases in sentences:

   impaired health tremulous hand
   appropriate measures charitable concessions

2. Pronounce:

   aerial frailty architect preliminary

3. What difference in meaning exists between **compliment** and **complement**?

Lesson 122

TEST ON USE OF THE DICTIONARY

This test should be completed in twenty minutes. Consult your dictionary for each answer. Points are to be deducted for each mistake.

1. *Definitions.*—Copy from the dictionary a short definition for each:

impetuous   manifest   eradicate   maltreat

2. *Spelling.*—Supply the omitted letter in each word:

mischiev—us   panor—ma   refer—ble   nonch—lant

3. *Parts of speech.*—What part of speech is each of these words?

salve   ennui   consummate   peremptory

4. *Synonyms.*—Give a synonym for each:

necessary   rudiment   virulent   miniature

5. *Syllabication.*—Divide each word into syllables:

proximity   illustrative   tremendous   domineer

6. *Accents.*—Divide into syllables and mark the accent of each word:

preferable   contemplate   despicable   comparable

7. *Principal parts.*—Give the past tense and past participle of each:

swim   ring   freeze   shine

8. *Foreign words.*—From what foreign language is each of these words taken? What is the meaning of each?

ibidem   rendezvous   alma mater   obbligato

9. *Word-pairs.*—What difference in meaning exists between these word-pairs?

revenge   vengeance   discreet   prudent

10. *Spelling.*—Which of these words double the "l" for the adjective and present participle?

marvel   cancel   imperil   libel

Lesson 123

TRUE OR FALSE TEST

delegate (*v.*)	convenience	pensive
comparative	obstinate	confusion
zealous	incident	inflict
deliberate (*v.*)	spacious	allege

A. A definition follows each of these twelve words. Some are correct; some are incorrect. Tell which are true and which are false.

delegate (*v.*)	To send an agent with authority; intrust.
comparative	Resulting from a comparison; relative.
zealous	Enthusiastic; eager.
deliberate (*v.*)	To free; release from fetters.
convenience	Accommodation; ease; comfort.
obstinate	Headstrong; not yielding to persuasion.
incident	An unexpected event, generally unfortunate.
spacious	Empty; small dimensions.
pensive	Sadly thoughtful; musing.
confusion	Tumult; disorder; perplexity.
allege	To produce as argument; affirm; declare.
inflict	To cause as if by striking; to impose punishment.

B. Is each of the bold-type words in the following sentences used correctly?

1. An attempt was made to **deliberate** the prisoner.
2. I wish you would visit me at your earliest **convenience**.
3. The old house had many **spacious** rooms.
4. Whom have you **delegated** to go to the convention?
5. She often seemed to be in a **pensive** mood.

C. Write the noun-form of:

delegate   obstinate   inflict   deliberate

D. Construct sentences with:

closed incident   **pensive** disposition

152

WORDS OF THE 3,000–4,000 POSITION
IN THORNDIKE'S LIST

abhor	pomp	induce	boundless
laurel	stale	remind	majestic
joyous	normal	quicken	obedience
array	obscure	inspire	meanwhile
invade	stalk	stately	reconcile
luster	muzzle	reject	prescribe
legion	obstacle	wholly	memorial
plane	patient	scent	sensible
adorn	impress	reform	occasional
mature	parch	waver	prominent
unity	cruelty	attorney	imperial
yawn	orient	startle	testimony
pious	idler	resume	utterance
amuse	impose	scout	principle
museum	arrest	warmth	temperate
mood	defy	ordain	weakness
woven	fiery	nickel	substitute
pillar	assert	scheme	vengeance
mutual	feign	oppress	composition
peril	denote	retreat	attractive
wretch	assign	lament	comprehend
vile	defect	involve	reverence
vivid	accord	resist	restaurant
wither	ideal	liberal	application
sullen	salute	mixture	correspond

Exercise

1. Construct sentences containing these words:

luster	impose	sensible	attractive
wither	lament	reconcile	vengeance

2. Pronounce:

museum	ideal	scheme	imperial

3. How does **comprehend** differ from **apprehend**?

4. Is there such a word as **nickle**?

153

WORDS REQUIRING CERTAIN PREPOSITIONS

agree with (*a person*):

The members of the club did not **agree with** me in regard to the purchase of a new home.

agree to (*a proposal*):

Do you think John will **agree to** my proposition?

agree upon (*a course*):

We finally **agreed upon** the arrangement of the furniture.

compare with (*in quality*):

Mr. Skehan's plan **compares** favorably **with** the one submitted by Mr. Jones.

differ with:

The members of the basketball team **differed with** their coach in regard to the style of play.

different from (*appearance*):

I am sure her dress is **different from** mine.

approve of:

The principal did not **approve of** the way in which the students were behaving.

accompanied by (*persons*):

The boy came to school **accompanied by** his mother.

accompanied with (*things*):

The music of the band was **accompanied with** great cheering from the victorious side.

absolve from:

The prisoner was **absolved from** all guilt.

abstinence from:

The doctor ordered **abstinence from** food for two days.

Caution

Different never takes the preposition **than.**

WORDS REQUIRING CERTAIN PREPOSITIONS

satisfied with:

We were not **satisfied with** the progress Katherine was making.

analogous to or **in:**

The case of Mr. George, who was very wealthy, is not **analogous to** your case.

originate in (*things*):

This idea **originated in** the fact that formerly such positions were not open to women.

originate with (*persons*):

The plan of admitting only problems into the book **originated with** Mr. Gilman.

correspond to (*things*):

My hat and suit **correspond** in color **to** yours.

correspond with (*persons*):

Jeannette **corresponds with** me steadily, and her letters are most interesting.

speak to (*casually*):

It was because I did not recognize you that I did not **speak to** you this morning.

speak with (*for a definite time*):

The last time Martin was **speaking with** me, he did not mention the fact that he was going away.

angry with (*persons*):

Mr. Jay never becomes **angry with** his employees for unavoidable mistakes.

angry at (*circumstances*):

The teacher was **angry at** John's tardiness today and kept him in after school.

parallel with or **to:**

The street you are speaking of runs **parallel with** (or **parallel to**) Joyce Avenue.

Lesson 127

WORDS REQUIRING CERTAIN PREPOSITIONS

sensible of:

I am **sensible of** the great favor you are conferring upon me.

part from (*persons*):

It was with deep regret that I **parted from** such kind friends.

part with (*things*):

These books are so interesting that I do not like to **part with** them.

oblivious of:

Mr. Albert became **oblivious of** the time and was half an hour late for his appointment.

ingratiate with or **into:**

He **ingratiated** himself **with** all about him.

Sir Roger did everything to **ingratiate** himself **into** the favor of the king.

accident of or **with:**

It was a mere **accident of** birth that he occupied the throne.

He had an **accident with** his motorcycle.

acquaintance with:

His speech showed that he had a great **acquaintance with** his subject.

addicted to:

It was commonly known that the leader was **addicted to** drink.

revenge upon or **for:**

He took **revenge upon** his enemy.

He took **revenge for** the injury he received.

prejudice against:

It has been proved that we had no **prejudice against** him.

synonymous with:

The name of Fagin, in "Oliver Twist," is **synonymous with** cruelty.

interpose between or **in:**

Why did you **interpose between** the combatants?

156

Lesson 128

LATIN ROOTS

Exercises

A. The words in this exercise are derived from the following Latin words:

anima	Life.	cedere (cessum)	To yield.
caput	Head.	ducere (ductum)	To lead.

Consult your dictionary for the meaning of each of the following words and for its relationship to the word-root:

animal	intercede	decapitate
capital	inanimate	accession
seduce	deduction	recapitulate
cede	antecedent	reanimate
captain	introduce	procession
concession	precipitate	conducive
cessation	intercession	inducement

B. The words in this exercise are derived from the following Latin words:

annus	Year.	fluere (fluxi)	To flow.
animus	Mind.	credere (creditum)	To believe.

Give the meaning of each word:

annual	unanimous	credulous
credence	biannual	magnanimous
fluent	credible	anniversary
influx	confluence	credential
fluctuate	animosity	centennial
incredulity	annuity	superfluous
biennial	creditor	circumfluent
affluence	influence	perennial

C. Give three English words which are derived from:

manus	Hand.	ponere (positum)	To place.
fortis	Brave.	jacere (jactum)	To throw.

Examples:

manual	fortitude	transpose	inject

157

Lesson 129

LATIN FORMS

The English pronunciations of certain Latin forms are given below:

extempore	(ĕks tĕm′pŏ rĕ)	Without study; impromptu.
alma mater	(ăl′mȧ mā′tēr)	One's college (*lit., "benign mother"*).
bona fide	(bō′nȧ fī′dĕ)	Genuine (*lit., "in good faith"*).
ad valorem	(ăd vă lō′rĕm)	Levied according to value (*as a customs duty*).

Read aloud:

1. He delivered a speech **extempore.**
2. Yale is my **alma mater.**
3. I understand that the agreement was not a **bona fide** one.
4. There is an **ad valorem** duty on diamonds that are brought to this country.

ex officio	(ĕks ŏ fĭ′shĭ ŏ)	By right of office.
de facto	(dĕ făk′tō)	Actual, in fact.
post-mortem	(pōst môr′tĕm)	After death.
ad infinitum	(ăd ĭn fĭ nī′tŭm)	Without end.

The above words are here used in sentences:

1. The mayor is the chairman **ex officio** of the Board of Education.
2. For a long time the **de facto** government in Mexico had to use drastic measures to enforce its laws.
3. The **post-mortem** autopsy revealed that the victim had been poisoned.
4. The work of God goes on **ad infinitum.**

Exercises

A. Explain the meanings of the bold-type Latin expressions:

1. On the tombstone was carved **"Requiescat in pace."**
2. The meeting adjourned **sine die.**
3. It is difficult to quote his speech **verbatim.**
4. Such **sub rosa** proceedings were condemned by the council.
5. Plenty of sleep is a **sine qua non** for good health.

B. To which of the above words are the following related?

fidelity	official	extemporize
infinity	factor	mortuary
faction	officiate	matriculate

158

TEST IX

(This test embraces material found in Lessons 112–128 inclusive.)

I. Which of these compounds do not require a hyphen?

stock room	railroad company
major general	self confidence
tailor made	ticket office

II. Write sentences containing the noun-form of each:

prudent	suspicious	turbulent
indolent	vigilant	hospitable

III. What are the correct meanings and usages of each?

agree to	differ with	angry at
agree upon	differ from	angry with
speak to	part from	originate in
speak with	part with	originate with

IV. What are the meanings of these Latin expressions?

bona fide	extempore
de facto	ad infinitum

V. Write two words derived from the following Latin words:

annus Year.   **fluere** To flow.   **credere** To believe.

VI. Construct sentences containing:

pensive	zealous	deliberate
justify	integrity	remonstrate

VII. Place in sentences:

imperative needs	fraudulent measures
heinous crime	expressive English
potent factor	mercenary motives
influential person	ludicrous remark

VIII. What is wrong with each sentence?

1. You aggravate me with your many questions.
2. Much good will be affected if you heed your brother's council.

IX. From what Latin roots are these words derived?

concede	intercede	recede
suppose	interpose	repose

159

Lesson 130

FRENCH WORDS

de luxe	(dĕ lüks′)	Luxurious, sumptuous.
buffet	(bŏŏ fā′)	Sideboard.
repertoire	(rĕp′ĕr twär)	List of dramas, operas, etc.
trousseau	(trōō′sō)	Bride's outfit of clothes.

The words in the preceding list are here used in sentences:

1. Mr. Hayward has recently purchased a **de luxe** edition of Shakespeare's works.
2. There is plenty of fruit upon the **buffet**.
3. A **buffet** lunch was served during the evening.
4. There was only one Shakespearean play in the actor's **repertoire**.
5. It required two trunks to carry her **trousseau**.

protégé	(prŏ′tȧ′zhā′)	One under another's protection.
chef d'œuvre	(shĕ dûvr′)	Masterpiece.
entree	(än′trā)	A side dish.
résumé	(rā zü mā′)	Summary.

1. He was the **protégé** of the great tennis player, Mr. Tilden.
2. Many believe that "The Age of Innocence" is Joshua Reynolds's **chef d'œuvre**.
3. The **entree** served at the banquet was very palatable.
4. The speaker gave a **résumé** of the political conditions existing in this country.

Exercise

1. The following words have been taken directly from the French language. Construct sentences with each of them.

depot	(dē′pō)	**tableau**	(tăb′lō)	**debut**	(dȧ bü′)
café	(kă fā′)	**garage**	(gȧ räzh′)	**prestige**	(prĕs tēzh′)
buffet	(bŏŏ fā′)	**regime**	(rā zhēm′)	**château**	(shȧ tō′)
melee	(mȧ lā′)	**matinee**	(măt ĭ nā′)	**apropos**	(ăp rȯ pō′)

2. Give a synonym for **résumé**.
3. How many pronunciations have the following words?

depot   buffet

Lesson 131

FOREIGN EXPRESSIONS

The foreign expressions in this list are often seen in English literature. Consult your dictionary to ascertain the meaning and the pronunciation of each.

nom de plume	ad libitum
pro et con	caveat emptor
gens d'armes	magnum opus
carte blanche	hoi polloi
Croix de guerre	nota bene
auf Wiedersehen	hors de combat
carpe diem	facsimile
bon voyage	laissez faire
multum in parvo	coup d'état
faux pas	sans souci
quo vadis	in statu quo
ne plus ultra	ex libris
savoir-faire	à-la-mode
au fait	esprit de corps
terra firma	mal de mer
honi soit qui mal y pense	sub rosa
en masse	pourboire
ex cathedra	pro tempore
bel-esprit	beau geste
per capita	sine qua non

Exercise

Some of the above expressions are here used in sentences:

1. The members were assessed ten dollars **per capita.**
2. This is a **facsimile** of John Hancock's signature.
3. The **esprit de corps** of our organization elicited much praise.
4. Honesty in business is a **sine qua non** for success.

WORDS OF THE 6,000–8,000 POSITION
IN THORNDIKE'S LIST

radius	qualify	integrity	instinctive
inspect	gravity	gigantic	fraternity
enter	indignity	prosecute	continuance
exult	forcible	iniquity	prohibition
supplant	quotient	corporal	dauntless
infamy	fealty	prophetic	insensible
forbade	surname	injunction	concealment
compile	intercept	grandeur	apparition
factor	radical	explosion	proprietor
surely	informal	infamous	complicate
infect	gaiety	competent	automatic
fraught	festive	defective	supplicate
surgeon	interpose	irrigate	ingratitude
infer	colonel	composure	accidental
frugal	gambol	defendant	involuntary
corps	applicant	temporal	exposition
defraud	invasion	credulous	annoyance
surmise	aquarium	ceaseless	inscription
infuse	beautify	investment	adjustment
filial	initial	carnival	continental
cavalry	arrogant	arbitrary	irresistible
ardor	comedian	certainty	anticipate
cheque	austere	authentic	criticise
bereft	befriend	circulate	illuminate
blight	audible	rampant	apprehension

Exercise

1. Use the words of this list in sentences.
2. What is the correct pronunciation of these words?

fealty	gaiety	colonel	gigantic
infamous	credulous	authentic	rampant

Lesson 133

WORDS OF THE 8,000–10,000 POSITION
IN THORNDIKE'S LIST

acquit	brevity	alacrity	benefactor
candor	adequate	candidacy	inimitable
adhere	imperil	decisive	abstinence
botany	caprice	inability	antiseptic
deface	delicacy	absorbent	captivate
accurate	impotent	casualty	inaccessible
conform	certify	foresight	ferocious
adjudge	indefinite	demeanor	adoration
abstract	aversion	inanimate	commodious
belated	amateur	auxiliary	gallantry
decade	clemency	conformity	incomparable
geyser	alienate	grotesque	modernize
amity	impudence	judicious	antagonist
crisis	classify	incidental	compensate
glutton	indefinite	harshness	granulate
confront	defensive	insinuate	hysterical
affront	headstrong	audacious	accumulate
fumble	jubilant	indictment	magnitude
ignore	insolent	comparable	indispensable
anarchy	legible	maturity	reluctance
gauge	jeopardy	remission	indifference
avert	minority	moralize	monotonous
illegal	reliance	compliance	remonstrate
inscribe	modify	rigorous	inhospitable
harass	odorous	oppressive	benevolence

Exercise

1. Use the words of this list in sentences.
2. What is the correct pronunciation of these words?

impotent	decade	jeopardy	demonstrate
indictment	comparable	inimitable	remonstrate

INDEX TO WORDS

SUBJECT INDEX